Marriage Matters Manual
Extraordinary Change through Ordinary Moments

Winston T. Smith

Curriculum Development: Michael Breece

Study Guide with Leader's Notes

New Growth Press
WWW.NEWGROWTHPRESS.COM

Marriage Matters Manual:
Extraordinary Change through Ordinary Moments
Study Guide with Leader's Notes

New Growth Press, Greensboro, NC 27404
Copyright © 2011 by Winston T. Smith
All rights reserved. Published 2011.

All Scripture quotations, unless otherwise indicated, are taken from the Holy Bible, New International Version®. NIV®. Copyright © 1973, 1978, 1984 by International Bible Society. Used by permission of Zondervan. All rights reserved.

Typesetting: Lisa Parnell, lparnell.com

ISBN (Print): 978-1-942572-73-2

Printed in the United States of America

25 24 23 22 21 20 19 18   4 5 6 7 8

Contents

Acknowledgments iv

Introduction 1

Unit 1: *Introduction to Marital Change* 3

Unit 2: *Worship Changes Marriages* 18

Unit 3: *You and Me and Marriage* 34

Unit 4: *Communication: Honesty and Oneness* 49

Unit 5: *Constructive Communication* 65

Unit 6: *Conflict: God Is Up to Something Good* 79

Unit 7: *Forgiveness* 96

Unit 8: *Building Intimacy* 116

Unit 9: *Marriage Roles* 133

Unit 10: *Keep Your Eyes on the Prize* 156

Leaders Guide 177

Acknowledgments

You would probably be surprised by the incredible amount of work required to create a useful study guide, even when your starting point is the finished manuscript of a book. I owe an enormous debt of gratitude to my co-laborers: Michael Breece, Barbara Juliani, and Nancy Winter. Their thoughtful and careful work transformed *Marriage Matters* into a companion workbook, a feat I could never have accomplished on my own. Of course, thanks to New Growth Press for having the vision to see that the very premise of *Marriage Matters: Extraordinary Change through Ordinary Moments* demands a workbook. Your dedication to helping others and not simply to selling books makes all the difference in the world. And special thanks go to the congregation of Bridge Community Church in Cheltenham, Pennsylvania, for volunteering the first group of couples to work through the manual. Your kind words and helpful feedback have been invaluable and are deeply appreciated.

Introduction

One of the important principles of *Marriage Matters* is that it is important to learn by doing. Of course, good information is indispensable to learning and *Marriage Matters* provides many important truths and principles that will help your marriage change through ordinary moments. But information alone isn't enough. If your marriage is going to grow you've actually got to put those truths and principles into practice. You might think of it like learning to drive. A book can tell you how to turn the ignition, put the car in gear, and explain the rules of the road, but you won't really know how to drive until you've actually gotten behind the wheel and driven. The *Marriage Matters Manual* is an opportunity for you to put what you learn in the book into practice, so that you grow in your ability to love well rather than just gaining more information about marriage.

This manual is carefully structured to promote an open and constructive exploration of the principles set forth in the book in a variety of ways. Each unit begins with a summary of key ideas contained in the unit and directs you to the relevant chapters of *Marriage Matters* that should be read in preparation for each unit. Once you have read the relevant portions of *Marriage Matters,* you and your spouse can then begin the unit as part of a small group study, marriage enrichment program, or even with the help of a marriage counselor or mentor. Throughout the unit you will be led through an exploration of each key idea by discussing what you've read, completing thought-provoking exercises, examining true-to-life vignettes, and studying relevant Bible passages. Finally, each unit ends by providing you with an exercise that will help you grow in your individual relationship with God, and a second exercise that will help you build your relationship with your spouse.

However, there is one critical ingredient that you will not find in *Marriage Matters* or in this manual which you must bring to this study: you must be more interested in learning how God would like to change you than in learning how to change your spouse. That can be hard to do, but if you're willing to prayerfully make that commitment, you can be certain that positive things will follow.

Here are some ways you can keep that commitment throughout the course:

- Focus on applying what you learn about your marriage to yourself. Make it your goal to learn to be a better spouse and allow God to work in your spouse's heart to see the things he or she needs to see.
- If in the course of this study conflicts occur between you and your spouse that can't be resolved, please ask a wise friend, pastor, counselor, or another couple whom you respect to meet with you and help you think through the issue together.
- Don't share your spouse's sins, perceived faults, or failures with the group. Be careful not to share incidents that put your spouse in a bad light or personal things that would be embarrassing to you or your spouse.
- Do share ways that you feel God is asking you to change and ask others to join you in praying for those things.

It is my hope and prayer that through the use of this study you will not only grow closer to your spouse, but to Christ himself, the one whose love our marriages are intended to reflect.

Unit 1

Introduction to Marital Change

KEY PASSAGE: 1 JOHN 4:7–12

KEY IDEAS:
1. We are prone to handle the ordinary moments of marriage on our own as if God were uninterested in the things that trouble us.
2. God is love, and when you find it hard to love, you need him all the more. A lack of love means you should not just look more closely at your marriage, but at yourself and at God. If you have any hope of having more love in your marriage, it's going to mean having more of God in your marriage.
3. Grace is another way of talking about God's love. It's more than a helping hand—it's God's love given to rescue us though we don't deserve it and have no hope of rescuing ourselves.
4. A relationship with God by his grace will always result in love expressed as grace toward our spouses even when it hurts.
5. Problems loving your spouse are only a symptom of a deeper problem: a lack of love for God and not grasping God's love for you expressed in the free gift of Jesus Christ.

TO PREPARE FOR THIS SESSION:

In *Marriage Matters* read Chapters 1 and 2 (pages 3–23), Chapter 16 (pages 239–251), and the first few pages in Chapter 17 (pages 253–259).

Lesson 1

OPENING ACTIVITY

Key Idea: We are prone to handle the ordinary moments of marriage on our own as if God were uninterested in the things that trouble us.

- *List some ordinary irritations and problems of marriage.*

- *Discuss what makes these things seem so ordinary.*

GOD AND LOVE

Key Idea: God is love, and when you find it hard to love, you need him all the more. A lack of love means you should not just look more closely at your marriage, but at yourself and at God. If you have any hope of having more love in your marriage, it's going to mean having more of God in your marriage.

The ordinary irritations and problems in marriage are often love problems—we don't feel loved or we are finding it hard to show love. The key passage, 1 John 4:7–12, defines love for us, so it is vitally important to the problems we face in our marriages.

Read 1 John 4:7–12 and discuss the questions that follow.

> ⁷Dear friends, let us love one another, for love comes from God. Everyone who loves has been born of God and knows God. ⁸Whoever does not love does not know God, because God is love. ⁹This is how God showed his love among us: He sent his one and only Son into the world that we might live through him. ¹⁰This is love: not that we loved God, but that he loved us and sent his Son as an atoning sacrifice for our sins. ¹¹Dear friends, since God so loved us, we also ought to love one another. ¹²No one has ever seen God; but if we love one another, God lives in us and his love is made complete in us.

1. *What does this passage teach about God?*

2. *How does God show his love to us?*

3. What does this passage teach about love?

4. Why are we to show love to one another?

5. What are some ways to apply these truths to marriage?

LOVE AND GRACE

Key Idea: Grace is another way of talking about God's love. It's more than a helping hand—it is God's love given to rescue us though we don't deserve it and have no hope of rescuing ourselves.

Read through this section and answer the questions below.

All that we have to learn about love in the passage from 1 John can be summed up in one word: grace. All of the ways that God has loved us through Jesus are expressions of grace. Grace basically means unearned or undeserved favor. God doesn't love us because we've earned it. In fact, because of our sin we deserve his rejection and judgment. When we first enter into relationship with God, we must acknowledge our inability to rescue ourselves from the brokenness and rebellion of sin and accept his love as an undeserved gift in Jesus. That's why, as John writes, Jesus came to be an "atoning sacrifice for our sins." He both earned God's favor and suffered our punishment for us. Now God's love is given to us when we place our trust in Jesus. It is an unearned gift.

Even so, Christians often have a narrow understanding of grace. We understand that we are saved by God's grace. But then we live our lives as if it is our duty to earn God's approval by trying our hardest to do what God requires of us, to live good lives, to be "good people." But the Bible says that we need God's unearned power and love all the time. Read the following description of two different views of God's grace:

> Two seventeenth-century theologians were debating on the nature of grace. One said that grace is like one parent guiding a toddler across the room to the other parent, who has an apple for the child. The nearby parent watches the youngster; if he almost falls, this parent will hold him for a moment so that he can still cross the room under his own power. But the other theologian had a different view. For him grace comes to us only in the discovery of our total helplessness. In his concept, we are like a caterpillar in a ring of fire. Deliverance can only come from above.*

If we are toddlers being steadied by a loving parent as needed, then grace is little more than a helping hand, but we are still largely

---

* Rose Marie Miller, *From Fear to Freedom: Living as Sons and Daughters of God* (Wheaton, IL: Harold Shaw Publishers, 1994), 4–5.

left to our own devices, relying on our own abilities. Let the second image sink in: a caterpillar in a ring of fire. It is a much better picture of grace. A caterpillar only crawls; its best efforts at salvation could only be dragging itself across consuming flames. A shove in the right direction only reinforces its own useless efforts and pushes it more quickly into the flames. It doesn't need help getting started; nor does it do any good to meet the caterpillar on the other side with a fire extinguisher. If the caterpillar is to escape the flames, deliverance must be total, and it must come from beyond the caterpillar. God, in the Bible, describes his grace as total deliverance for helpless people (Ephesians 2:5–9).

Discuss the following questions:
1. *How would you describe the difference between receiving a "helping hand" and being utterly dependent on God?*

2. *Has your marriage been based mainly on your own ability or upon God's grace? Explain.*

3. *What causes you to sometimes ignore God and try to do life on your own?*

GRACE AND MARRIAGE

Key Idea: A relationship with God by his grace will always result in love expressed as grace toward our spouses even when it hurts.

Read the following account of one ordinary moment in my marriage.

> I could feel my blood pressure rising. With every passing moment I was getting more and more angry. It was 2:30. My son's baseball practice was at 3:00, my daughter had a birthday party at 4:00, and I had to lead a Bible study at 5:00. What's more, my wife was not answering her cell phone. I'd been calling her every few minutes since 1:00, and now it was almost 2:30. She should have been home long ago. She knew what was on the schedule, and she'd assured me she'd be home on time. How was I going to prepare my Bible study with all this taxiing to do? Did she not care that I was juggling this all by myself?
> My anger mounted as I pictured her chatting with friends, while her cell phone, set to vibrate, hummed away unnoticed in her handbag. I resigned myself to plan B: all three kids would come to baseball practice, and the girls would play in an empty part of the field, while I sat in the van and worked on the Bible study. There would be

distractions. I would want to watch practice, and the girls would need to be watched. They would get bored and start asking for things. It was not ideal, but it would have to do.

I barked orders at the kids to get ready to go. There were a hundred questions: "Where's Mommy?" "Why do we have to go to baseball practice?" "Am I going to miss my party?" "Where are my shoes?" "Can we stop at the store and get a snack?" Every question was a frustrating reminder that I shouldn't have to be dealing with this.

Just then the phone rang, "Win, have you been trying to call me?"

"Yeeeeees," I replied, injecting as much sarcasm as possible into that one word. "I have to get Gresham to practice and Charlotte to her birthday party, and I'm not prepared for Bible study. Why haven't you answered your phone?"

"I didn't hear it ringing in my bag. I'm so sorry. I'll be home in a few minutes. I just couldn't get away as soon as I thought I could."

Instead of waiting for Kim to return and let her deliver our son to practice, I loaded the kids into the car and took them myself. When I returned home, fifteen minutes later, Kim was there wondering why I hadn't waited for her.

She retreated to a safe distance. I sat alone staring at the kitchen table. I was more than just annoyed; I was fuming. Beneath the anger I also felt embarrassed and ashamed. Part of me felt justified in my anger, while another part of me wondered why I'd gotten so worked up. Irritation would be understandable, but anger?

My response was out of proportion, and I knew it. I soon realized that part of my frustration stemmed from the fact that this feeling was familiar, even ordinary. How often have I been angry with Kim because I felt that she hasn't stopped to think about me? And how often have I had the same pouty reaction and witnessed the same destructive result? I was tired of reliving this moment, tired of having the same old argument and getting the same old result.

1. *What makes this an ordinary moment?*

2. *What would need to happen for this moment to be redeemed by God? How could the husband and wife in this story have shown grace to each other?*

SOMETHING TO THINK ABOUT:

When we think about our relationship with God, grace is essentially a passive verb: God has done and is doing something for us that we don't deserve and can't possibly do for ourselves. Grace requires our utter dependence on Christ. But grace is a feature of love and, therefore, something that must be reflected in our relationships with others, especially our spouses. In marriage, grace is more of an active verb; it is something that we must actively do or practice toward others. Just as God gives his love to us when we least deserve it, we need his help to love our spouses in the same way. Relationship with God by his grace will always result in love expressed as grace toward our spouses even when it hurts.

Homework for Unit 1

Key Idea: Problems loving your spouse are only a symptom of a deeper problem: a lack of love for God and not grasping God's love for you expressed in the free gift of Jesus Christ.

Complete this homework before the next session. Record your thoughts and responses below and bring it to the group meeting.

BUILDING YOUR RELATIONSHIP WITH GOD

On your own, read Hebrews 4:14–16 and answer the questions that follow.

> [14]Therefore, since we have a great high priest who has gone through the heavens, Jesus the Son of God, let us hold firmly to the faith we profess. [15]For we do not have a high priest who is unable to sympathize with our weaknesses, but we have one who has been tempted in every way, just as we are—yet was without sin. [16]Let us then approach the throne of grace with confidence, so that we may receive mercy and find grace to help us in our time of need.

1. *The high priest represented the people before God and offered the sacrifices for sin. What does it mean for us that Jesus has the role of our high priest? (See Hebrews 2:14–18; 5:1.)*

2. *Hebrews 5:1 says a high priest represents men "in matters related to God." Marriage is a matter related to God. Therefore, you have a high priest who is concerned about your marriage and who*

represents you as a married couple before the Father. What then does the writer of Hebrews encourage you to do?

3. *According to Hebrews 4:15, what is Jesus' response to your weaknesses?*

4. *Write a prayer expressing to God your weaknesses, fears, and doubts. Try to verbalize what you believe and what you think you need from God.*

BUILDING YOUR RELATIONSHIP WITH EACH OTHER

As a couple read the following passage and discuss the questions that follow.

> [16]Now a man came up to Jesus and asked, "Teacher, what good thing must I do to get eternal life?"
>
> [17]"Why do you ask me about what is good?" Jesus replied. "There is only One who is good. If you want to enter life, obey the commandments."
>
> [18]"Which ones?" the man inquired.
>
> Jesus replied, "'Do not murder, do not commit adultery, do not steal, do not give false testimony, [19]honor your father and mother', and 'love your neighbor as yourself.'"
>
> [20]"All these I have kept," the young man said. "What do I still lack?"
>
> [21]Jesus answered, "If you want to be perfect, go, sell your possessions and give to the poor, and you will have treasure in heaven. Then come, follow me."
>
> [22]When the young man heard this, he went away sad, because he had great wealth. (Matthew 19:16–22)

1. *Was the young man wrong to ask Jesus about what is good? What point do you think Jesus was trying to make with his answer?*

2. *In response to the young man's second question (vs. 18), which commands does Jesus highlight? What do these commands have in common and why do you think Jesus highlights them?*

3. *The rich young man seems to have a genuine interest in being righteous, but Jesus points out a blind spot in his sincere heart. What blind spot does Jesus reveal?*

4. *What is Jesus saying about true religion or spirituality?*

5. *What can we deduce about the young man's true interest based on his final response to Jesus' answers?*

SOMETHING TO THINK ABOUT:

We know that God cares about our "spiritual" life—our prayers, church attendance, and Bible reading—but our marriages don't really seem to fall into this category. The command, "Love your neighbor as yourself," reminds us that every human interaction, every marital interaction, is a spiritual matter. Think about it: your spouse is your most immediate neighbor. The way you treat your spouse, then, reveals how seriously you take God's command and God himself. "Love your neighbor" is a command from God. Your obedience or disobedience is a window into your relationship with him. Problems loving your spouse are only a symptom of the true problem: whether or not you love God.

1. *Take turns describing one or two ordinary events in your marriage and how you handled them.*

2. *In light of God's commitment to redemption how could you have handled them differently?*

3. *Share with each other one way you have seen God's grace at work in your life and marriage.*

Pray together. Thank God for the ways you have seen his grace in your marriage. Invite God to continue his work in you. If you are doing this study as part of a larger group, pray for the other participants.

BEFORE THE NEXT SESSION:
In *Marriage Matters*, read Chapters 3 and 4 (pages 25–55).

Unit 2

Worship Changes Marriages

KEY PASSAGE: PSALM 115:3–13

KEY IDEAS:

1. The question isn't *whether* we worship, but *what* we worship.
2. We become like what we worship.
3. Worshiping God means having a relationship with him.
4. What we pursue is not always bad in and of itself. It becomes bad when we want it too much and it eclipses God, who alone deserves our worship.

TO PREPARE FOR THIS SESSION:

In *Marriage Matters* read Chapters 3 and 4 (pages 25–55).

Lesson 2

OPENING

- *Last week we learned that our relationship with our spouse is a window into what? Explain your answer.*

- *What can redeem and transform an ordinary marriage?*

- *Share briefly something you learned from doing the homework this week.*

- *If you feel comfortable doing so, share a way that you have seen God's grace at work in your marriage this week.*

WHAT DO YOU WORSHIP?

Key Idea: The question isn't *whether* we worship, but *what* we worship.

Read Psalm 71 and complete the exercises that follow.

> ¹In you, O Lord, I have taken refuge; let me never be put to shame. ²Rescue me and deliver me in your righteousness; turn your ear to me and save me. ³Be my rock of refuge, to which I can always go; give the command to save me, for you are my rock and my fortress. ⁴Deliver me, O my God, from the hand of the wicked, from the grasp of evil and cruel men.
> ⁵For you have been my hope, O Sovereign Lord, my confidence since my youth. ⁶From birth I have relied on you; you brought me forth from my mother's womb. I will ever praise you. ⁷I have become like a portent to many, but you

are my strong refuge. ⁸My mouth is filled with your praise, declaring your splendor all day long.

⁹Do not cast me away when I am old; do not forsake me when my strength is gone. ¹⁰For my enemies speak against me; those who wait to kill me conspire together. ¹¹They say, "God has forsaken him; pursue him and seize him, for no one will rescue him." ¹²Be not far from me, O God; come quickly, O my God, to help me. ¹³May my accusers perish in shame; may those who want to harm me be covered with scorn and disgrace.

¹⁴But as for me, I will always have hope; I will praise you more and more. ¹⁵My mouth will tell of your righteousness, of your salvation all day long, though I know not its measure. ¹⁶I will come and proclaim your mighty acts, O Sovereign Lord; I will proclaim your righteousness, yours alone. ¹⁷Since my youth, O God, you have taught me, and to this day I declare your marvelous deeds. ¹⁸Even when I am old and gray, do not forsake me, O God, till I declare your power to the next generation, your might to all who are to come.

¹⁹Your righteousness reaches to the skies, O God, you who have done great things. Who, O God, is like you? ²⁰Though you have made me see troubles, many and bitter, you will restore my life again; from the depths of the earth you will again bring me up. ²¹You will increase my honor and comfort me once again.

²²I will praise you with the harp for your faithfulness, O my God; I will sing praise to you with the lyre, O Holy One of Israel. ²³My lips will shout for joy when I sing praise to you—I, whom you have redeemed. ²⁴My tongue will tell of your righteous acts all day long, for those who wanted to harm me have been put to shame and confusion. (Psalm 71)

1. *Circle the words that describe God's role in the psalmist's life.*

2. *Underline words that describe qualities of God (don't be afraid to underline words that are already circled).*

3. Which of the circled words/phrases do you most identify with in your relationship with God?

SOMETHING TO THINK ABOUT:

We are accustomed to separating life into the spiritual and the unspiritual, handing the spiritual things over to God and managing the rest by ourselves. Marriage may be one of those areas that we like to manage on our own. However, consider Jesus' words: "'Love the Lord your God with all your heart and with all your soul and with all your mind.' This is the first and greatest commandment" (Matthew 22:37).

Is there any part of life that falls outside of your heart, mind, soul, and strength? This command makes it clear: God should be at the center of it all. This command breaks down the barriers we erect between the spiritual and unspiritual, between God and all of the areas of life we like to keep to ourselves. *Everything* we do is supposed to be guided by our love for God—our every action is an act of devotion to him.

This understanding of worship exposes us all as worshipers who have gone astray. The question isn't whether or not you will worship; the question is who or what you will worship.

This week at home you will begin to discover and identify those things you put at the center of your life instead of God (the Bible calls these things "idols"). Idols are things you want so much that you make them more important than God. An idol can also be something you use to protect yourself from what you fear instead of looking to God for your safety. But let's first look more closely at why the focus of your worship is so critical.

WORSHIP ALWAYS CHANGES YOU

Key Idea: We become like what we worship.

Read the passage from Psalm 115:3–13 and discuss the questions that follow.

> ³Our God is in heaven; he does whatever pleases him. ⁴But their idols are silver and gold, made by the hands of men. ⁵They have mouths, but cannot speak, eyes, but they cannot see; ⁶they have ears, but cannot hear, noses, but they cannot smell; ⁷they have hands, but cannot feel, feet, but they cannot walk; nor can they utter a sound with their throats. ⁸Those who make them will be like them, and so will all who trust in them.
>
> ⁹O house of Israel, trust in the LORD—he is their help and shield. ¹⁰O house of Aaron, trust in the LORD—he is their help and shield. ¹¹You who fear him, trust in the LORD—he is their help and shield. ¹²The LORD remembers us and will bless us: He will bless the house of Israel, he will bless the house of Aaron, ¹³he will bless those who fear the LORD—small and great alike.

1. *What are some characteristics of idols?*

2. *What is the danger of worshiping idols?*

3. *What is the effect of true worship?*

Reread the account of one ordinary moment in a marriage from the "Grace and Marriage" section of Lesson 1.

Discuss the following questions:

1. *Based on his reaction to the situation, what do you think is the husband's idol?*

2. What do you think he really wants?

3. What effect does idol worship have on him?

Now read what I learned about myself from that ordinary moment in my marriage:

> My response revealed an idol in my own heart—acceptance or approval. I wanted to do a good job with the Bible study, but I also work hard to be liked by my wife, Kim. After all, I was taking care of the kids on a Saturday so she could enjoy her friends. Didn't I deserve some credit for that? When I perceive myself as overlooked and ignored it feels as if all my effort is for nothing. Usually I am good at getting others to like me. When my wife does not fall in line, I get angry. In my anger I want to punish her for not noticing how hard I am working for her affirmation, approval, and affection.
>
> That Saturday, when I chose acceptance as my god I did so because I believed it would bring me life: joy, peace, and happiness. And it seemed to work, at least for a while. But over time, just as Psalm 115 predicts, I found it less and less

effective, and eventually found that I had less of the very things that I want. I didn't feel alive and free; I felt paralyzed. I didn't know what to say or do. I was trapped by my own strategy. Approval doesn't offer any solutions for anger. Idols bring death in exactly the way the psalmist describes. As I trained my eye to look for approval, I began to lose my ability to notice anything but its presence or absence. As I trained my ear to listen for the sounds of affirmation and praise, I became tone deaf to other important sounds, and even the most helpful and well-meaning criticism became unbearable. I chose an idol that I thought would bring me life, but instead I found that my life became flatter and flatter, reduced to the harsh monochrome reality of experiencing only acceptance and rejection.

WORSHIP IS MORE THAN KNOWING

Key Idea: Worshiping God means having a relationship with him.

As Psalm 115 tells us, idols simply cannot give us what we really need or deliver us from the hard things of life. But God invites us to turn away from trusting in idols, to seek his forgiveness and trust him. The Bible tells us that God is our "help and shield," the one who will forgive us and bless us. In particular, the Bible tells us that Jesus knows our temptations and hardships so we can go to him in prayer and "receive mercy and find grace to help us in our time of need" (Hebrews 4:16b).

Read Jesus' words in the following passage and then answer the questions that follow.

> "Remain in me, and I will remain in you. No branch can bear fruit by itself; it must remain in the vine. Neither can you bear fruit unless you remain in me. I am the vine; you are the branches. If a man remains in me and I in him, he will bear much fruit; apart from me you can do nothing." (John 15:4–5)

1. *Jesus is saying that we bear fruit according to what we are connected to. What are you connected to? (What things are most important to you? What do you look forward to doing? What brings you joy? What do you try to avoid at all costs?)*

2. *In Galatians 5:22–23, Paul describes the fruit of the Spirit as "love, joy, peace, patience, kindness, goodness, faithfulness, gentleness and self-control." According to Jesus, what is required to bear good fruit?*

3. *Using practical examples describe what it means to "remain" in Christ?*

SOMETHING TO THINK ABOUT:

Remaining in Christ is not just spending time with him but also obeying his instructions. When we choose not to obey, we sin and sin separates us from the Vine. Therefore worship is more than just knowing something; it also requires doing something. You can be certain that in marriage you will often do the right thing before you realize there is any benefit to it. Fruit doesn't grow overnight. And sometimes you don't *really* understand something until you *try* to do it. Sometimes we don't understand as much as we think we do until we actually take action. Growing in your marriage and in your relationship with God works the same way. You need to be willing to take action in order to change, even to understand what you need to learn.

Homework for Unit 2

Key Idea: What we pursue is not always bad in and of itself. It becomes bad when we want it too much and it eclipses God, who alone deserves our worship.

Complete this homework before the next session. Record your thoughts and responses below and bring it to the group meeting.

BUILDING YOUR RELATIONSHIP WITH GOD

On your own, read the following pages and complete all the activities and questions.

What keeps me from loving/worshiping God?

Some idols are easy to spot—we know they are wrong because God speaks directly about them in the Bible (for example, lust for someone who is not your spouse). But other idols are not so easy to identify because they are things that don't start out wrong, but become idols when we want them more than we want to love and serve God.

Think of five good things that are important to you in marriage, and list them below in the left column. Try to imagine what it looks like when any one of those things becomes too important to you, an idol. What would you do to have that thing or to avoid losing it? List those things in the right column.

Things That Are Important to Me	How I Act When They Become Idols
Example: RESPECT	BECOME SENSITIVE TO CRITICISM; ANGRILY ATTACK

We all have a natural inclination to love ourselves more than God. This is idolatry. Idolatry is the activity of worshiping *anything* other than God. Our most natural inclinations—seeking comfort, refuge, hoping, relying, etc.—are the behaviors of worship. The most insidious of idols are the ones we can't see—the ones we erect in our hearts.

You probably have specific idols that have a tendency to rule your heart and turn your worship away from God. Rate yourself on the following items. Don't overanalyze yourself. These are common, but not all-inclusive, symptoms that can reveal what may be happening in our hearts.

28 *Unit 2: Worship Changes Marriages*

Rate each of the following statements:
1–almost never, 2–sometimes, 3–more often than not, 4–to a great extent

1. ___ I become anxious when facing the unknown.
2. ___ I become anxious when faced with being alone or excluded.
3. ___ I do whatever is necessary to avoid stress.
4. ___ I become anxious at the possibility of failure or rejection.
5. ___ I become anxious when not in control.
6. ___ I fear my weaknesses/sins being exposed.
7. ___ I fear something bad will happen.
8. ___ I become defensive or hurt when criticized.
9. ___ I strongly dislike having to make sacrifices.
10. ___ I worry about not being the best.
11. ___ It is important to me that I feel respected.
12. ___ It is important to me that I feel accepted.
13. ___ It is important to me that I feel safe.
14. ___ It is important to me that I have "me time."
15. ___ It is important to me that I am a hard worker.
16. ___ I make decisions based on what will keep me from showing any faults or weaknesses.
17. ___ I make decisions based on what will please others.
18. ___ I make decisions regardless of others.
19. ___ I make decisions based on what will bring results.
20. ___ I make decisions based on what feels good.
21. ___ I make decisions based on what will require the least amount of responsibility.
22. ___ I either "shut down" or panic when bad things happen.
23. ___ I feel angry or anxious when I am unable to do anything.
24. ___ I will do or say whatever is necessary to get what I want.
25. ___ I will become defensive when others place expectations on me.
26. ___ I am easily offended by the actions or words of others.
27. ___ I feel inadequate or insignificant when not recognized by others.
28. ___ I base my identity on the opinions of others.
29. ___ I base my identity on what I accomplish.
30. ___ I base my identity on winning or positions of power.

A. *Add up the score you gave yourself on the following numbers:*
   1, 6, 7, 13, 16, 22 _____

B. *Add up the score you gave yourself on the following numbers:*
   2, 8, 12, 17, 26, 28 _____

C. *Add up the score you gave yourself on the following numbers:*
   3, 9, 14, 20, 21, 25 _____

D. *Add up the score you gave yourself on the following numbers:*
   4, 10, 15, 19, 27, 29 _____

E. *Add up the score you gave yourself on the following numbers:*
   5, 11, 18, 23, 24, 30 _____

Circle the numbers in A–E that you scored as a "3" or "4."

We all are driven by different desires: power, belonging, security, comfort, or significance. It isn't wrong to want approval, or to enjoy comfort, or even acknowledge the value of power. Often, we aren't aware of how idolatry is affecting us because what we are pursuing isn't a bad thing. However, it becomes a bad thing when we attach too much importance to it and seek it for selfish purposes. For example, it's natural to want approval, but when getting approval becomes too important to you it overshadows your love for God and your spouse. So idols can be things that are inherently bad, like an adulterous relationship, but the ones that often bedevil us the most are the ones that we've convinced ourselves are good, but become bad when they become too important to us and are driven by selfishness.

Identify the letter(s) you scored highest on and the ones you scored the most 3s and 4s on. Read the corresponding descriptions below and think about whether they accurately describe you. There is a good chance at least one of these areas can tend to take prominence in your life and lead you away from worshiping God alone.

Match your highest score with the description below.

A. You fear the possibility of anything bad happening—health problems, loss of financial security, a broken relationship, having your faults and weaknesses exposed—and therefore you often fear the unknown. Your decisions are often based on what will maintain the status quo and keep you safe. When things begin going bad, you feel anxious or depressed and you may panic, shut down, or run away. You dislike being singled out. The idol that may rule your heart is a desire for **security**.

B. You fear being alone or excluded; you wrestle with feelings of jealousy in your relationships; you can quickly feel offended by what others do or say; you make decisions based on what will please others and make them like you; you may avoid conflict or avoid others for fear they will reject or judge you. The idol that may rule your heart is a need for **acceptance** or belonging.

C. You fear stress and dislike anything that requires too much work, responsibility, or high expectations; you avoid anything that disrupts your plans and will become angry when your plans are interfered with; you avoid having to make sacrifices; you make decisions based on what feels good. The idol that may rule your heart is the desire for **comfort**.

D. You have the tendency to be task oriented and will avoid people if they prevent you from completing a task; you enjoy recognition; you can become defensive at criticism; you want to feel significant by what you achieve; you may fear failure or imperfection. The idol that may rule your heart is the drive for **achievement**, success, or significance.

E. You fear not being in control; you are driven by the chance to win or to have a position of power or responsibility; you can become angry or anxious when others try to control you; you are willing to be manipulative to get what you want; you strongly dislike being wrong or being asked to back down. The idol that may rule your heart is the need for **power** or control.

After considering these symptoms of idolatry, what did you learn or reconfirm about your own heart?

Ask for God's forgiveness for turning to idols. Remember, God's grace is undeserved favor. He won't reject you. He gives grace to all who seek his forgiveness and help as they trust in Jesus.

BUILDING YOUR RELATIONSHIP WITH EACH OTHER

As a couple, spend time together reading the following pages, discussing any questions, and completing the activities.

Share/discuss with your spouse what tends to fight for rule of your heart. Does your spouse agree? Confess your sin to each other and ask for forgiveness.

What attributes or qualities of God can you try to remember that will help you fight against this potential becoming the focus of your heart? What passages of Scripture will help you remember this attribute? How will remembering this attribute help you? Fill out the chart below following the example given.

Potential Idol	What Is God Like?	Scripture	How It Helps Me
Power/control	God is sovereign	Eph. 1:11: He works out everything in conformity to the purpose of his will.	I can let go of being in control because God is in control; nothing happens apart from God's will.

32 *Unit 2: Worship Changes Marriages*

Potential Idol	What Is God Like?	Scripture	How It Helps Me

Serving others is also an act of worship toward God. Do something this week to serve each other. Do something you do not normally do: prepare dinner or lunch, work outside, watch the children so your spouse can do something special, etc.

BEFORE THE NEXT SESSION:

In *Marriage Matters*, read Chapters 5 and 6 (pages 57–91).

Unit 3

You and Me and Marriage

KEY PASSAGES: GENESIS 1:26–28;
PHILIPPIANS 2:1–18

KEY IDEAS:
1. God designed marriage to image the unity and love that exists among Father, Son, and Holy Spirit and the unity and love he has with his people.
2. Sometimes what we think of as love is, in fact, manipulation. We treat our spouse like an object whose sole purpose is to give us what we want: rewarding them if they give us what we want, punishing them if they don't.
3. Honoring your spouse is a critical ingredient of love. It includes three things: understanding that your spouse belongs to God, working to help your spouse grow, and being willing to learn from him or her.
4. Analyzing patterns of manipulation helps us identify the desires and fears that we are serving when we fail to love our spouses.

TO PREPARE FOR THIS SESSION:
In *Marriage Matters*, read Chapters 5 and 6 (pages 57–91).

Lesson 3

OPENING REVIEW

We are all worshipers who have gone astray. Share one potential idol you identified from your time together and share what attribute of God and passage of Scripture will help you keep that idol from being the focus of your heart.

THE CREATION AND PURPOSE OF MARRIAGE

Key Idea: God designed marriage to image the unity and love that exists among Father, Son, and Holy Spirit and the unity and love he has with his people.

Read the following passage and discuss the questions.

> [26]Then God said, "Let us make man in our image, in our likeness, and let them rule over the fish of the sea and the birds of the air, over the livestock, over all the earth, and over all the creatures that move along the ground." [27]So God created man in his own image, in the image of God he created him; male and female he created them. [28]God blessed them and said to them, "Be fruitful and increase in number; fill the earth and subdue it. Rule over the fish of the sea and the birds of the air and over every living creature that moves on the ground." (Genesis 1:26–28)

1. *What does it mean to "image" God? In what ways does God want us to image him?*

2. If God exists as three Persons, and we were created in his image, what is the problem with being alone?

3. How should that inform our understanding of God's purpose of marriage?

4. Many of the attributes and characteristics of God are on display in relationships. List some of God's characteristics that we should image as we interact with others.

Read the following passage and discuss the questions.

> [25]Husbands, love your wives, just as Christ loved the church and gave himself up for her [26]to make her holy,

cleansing her by the washing with water through the word, [27]and to present her to himself as a radiant church, without stain or wrinkle or any other blemish, but holy and blameless. (Ephesians 5:25–27)

1. *According to this passage, what are our marriages supposed to look like?*

2. *How would you describe the way Christ loves the church?*

SOMETHING TO THINK ABOUT:

Are *you* willing to love motivated by what is truly best for the other person and willing to give everything to accomplish it?

Read the following passages and discuss the questions.

> [20]...But if you suffer for doing good and you endure it, this is commendable before God. [21]To this you were called, because Christ suffered for you, leaving you an example, that you should follow in his steps. "He committed no sin, and

no deceit was found in his mouth." [23]When they hurled their insults at him, he did not retaliate; when he suffered, he made no threats. Instead, he entrusted himself to him who judges justly. [24]He himself bore our sins in his body on the tree, so that we might die to sins and live for righteousness; by his wounds you have been healed. [25]For you were like sheep going astray, but now you have returned to the Shepherd and Overseer of your souls. (1 Peter 2:20b–25)

Wives, in the same way be submissive to your husbands so that, if any of them do not believe the word, they may be won over without words by the behavior of their wives, when they see the purity and reverence of your lives.
(1 Peter 3:1–2)

Husbands, in the same way be considerate as you live with your wives, and treat them with respect as the weaker partner and as heirs with you of the gracious gift of life, so that nothing will hinder your prayers. (1 Peter 3:7)

1. *What is Peter's main idea in verses 20–25?*

2. *What was the purpose of Christ's suffering?*

3. How did Jesus respond to suffering?

4. What does it mean when Peter says husbands and wives should act "in the same way" in their marriages?

WHOSE PURPOSE DOES YOUR MARRIAGE SERVE?

Key Idea: Sometimes what we think of as love is, in fact, manipulation. We treat our spouse like an object whose sole purpose is to give us what we want: rewarding them if they give us what we want, punishing them if they don't.

Understanding that our spouses are made in the image of God means we must not manipulate them, treating them as objects that exist for our own purposes. We must honor and respect them as God's possessions. As image bearers, it's our responsibility to love them as God loves us.

Evaluate the following two scenarios and discuss how manipulation is taking place.

Scenario A

Once again, James left a wet towel in the middle of the bedroom floor. It wouldn't be so bad except he leaves things lying around all over the place, and he has promised many times not to leave his towel on the floor. There was no solution. If Sonya left it there, it would become a permanent fixture in their room. If she confronted him about it, he would usually let out a big sigh and then pick it up. Sonya was tired of picking it up and tired of confronting him about it. This time she would not speak to James at all until he figured it out on his own.

Scenario B

Charles surprised Jessica with a beautiful bouquet of flowers and announced, "I made reservations at Star's for dinner tonight."

Jessica's shoulders drooped. "He knows I hate being out on a weeknight because I have to be up very early to go to work," she thought to herself. "Honey, thank you, but you know I don't like going out on weeknights. I have told you that before."

Charles' smile turned to a quick grimace. "It's just dinner," he said. "We'll be back early."

Jessica knew they wouldn't be back early. "No, I can't."

"I don't know why I bother trying to spend time with you," Charles snapped.

If our marriages are going to grow in love, then they must be built on a foundation of honoring our spouses, treating them as image bearers—people who have value whether we're getting what we want or not. If we only show them favor to get what we want, even if the things we want are good things, we will be practicing a form of manipulation and actually sucking the love out of our marriages.

"CONSIDER OTHERS BETTER THAN YOURSELVES"

Key Idea: Honoring your spouse is a critical ingredient of love. It includes three things:

- **Understanding that your spouse belongs to God**
- **Working to help your spouse grow**
- **Being willing to learn from him or her**

If manipulation describes the attitude that violates love, then honor is the attitude that fosters love and leads to acts of real love. Honor means regarding others as having value and importance. In fact, most often, the Bible encourages us not just to see others as our peers, but to give them more honor than we give ourselves.

In Paul's letter to the Philippian church he writes, "Do nothing out of selfish ambition or vain conceit, but in humility consider others better than yourselves" (Philippians 2:3). Often when we manipulate our spouse we take on the role of their judge and master. We interact with them as if they exist to meet our desires or to protect us from our fears. When we treat our spouse with honor we are more likely to take on the role as caretaker and steward.

Discuss the following questions:

1. *How does God treat us? How do we know that we are valuable to him?*

2. *What are some practical ways that Sonya could honor James and James could honor Sonya in Scenario A?*

3. *What are some practical ways that Charles could honor Jessica and Jessica could honor Charles in Scenario B?*

Homework for Unit 3

Key Idea: Analyzing patterns of manipulation helps us identify the desires and fears that we are serving when we fail to love our spouses.

Complete this homework before the next session. Record your thoughts and responses below and bring it to the group meeting.

BUILDING YOUR RELATIONSHIP WITH GOD

On your own, read the following pages and complete all the activities and questions.

Patterns of Manipulation

Taking the time to identify the typical ways that you manipulate your spouse can be a real advantage to growing in love. There are some typical patterns or styles of manipulation. The one you favor provides clues to the heart issues or idols that drive you.

Moving toward others. Sometimes getting the things you want or avoiding the things you fear means you need to get more out of the people in your life. Say, for example, you crave approval, affection, intimacy, belonging, or safety. Those are things you get from other people—and sometimes it takes lots of other people to get what you crave. So you do things that will bring people into your world. If acceptance is one of your chief desires, you may use any number of various strategies to draw others in. You may hone a great sense of humor, be an extravagant gift giver, a ready hand to help others out. On the other hand, if you don't have much confidence in your ability to gain others' acceptance you may employ more "negative" strategies like pouting, withdrawing, becoming clingy, or even taking more desperate measures like harming yourself.

Moving away from others. Sometimes acquiring the things you want or avoiding the things you fear requires *less* of the people in your life. Some people find that peace, control, perfection, order, and safety are more easily secured by having fewer people in their world or exercising tight control over those who are there. Some of the same "positive" strategies mentioned above can also serve as a way of carefully controlling or limiting other people's access to your world. For instance, a sharp wit can be an invitation to someone's company or a way to jab at those you want to keep at a distance.

Moving against others. Sometimes acquiring the things you want or avoiding the things you fear requires you to move *against* others. If you desire superiority, control, success, or power, you'll probably be moving against the wishes of others in order to get them—or to demonstrate that you have them. Making sure that my plans succeed and yours fail can give me a sense that my plans are better than yours and so I am better than you. When you fail I feel more successful, so I take steps to ensure that you fail. Strategies for moving against others can be as elaborate as dominating vacation plans or as small as nit-picking another person's grammar.

Self-evaluation

Answer the following questions:

1. Do you respond differently in different relationships?

2. Do you have a typical style in your marriage?

Using the Patterns as a Starting Point

You may have noticed that some of the listed desires and fears occur in more than one pattern of manipulation (safety and control, for example). The desires and fears listed under each pattern are more typical for those patterns, but it's important to keep in mind that each pattern can serve any and every desire depending on how it's employed. The motives suggested above for each pattern provide a typical starting point for understanding what motivations might lie beneath your relational patterns or those of your spouse.

It's also very important to understand that the above patterns don't always suggest sinful manipulation. Love itself sometimes moves toward others, sometimes away from others, and sometimes against others. There's more to love than drawing near. Sometimes love requires you to move away from one you love so as not to participate in evil. Or you may need to create distance in an abusive relationship. Love may even call you to move against someone you love—not to that person's detriment, but in challenging sinful behavior or to protect others. In marriage, love will, at times, require you to say no or otherwise challenge your spouse just as God challenges us when we need it.

It's critical to start with an honest look at your own attitudes. I've seen many couples stumble in their beginning attempts to change, because (without realizing it) they are expressing an attitude that undercuts every effort to love. When you look at your spouse, do you see someone who *should* be loved, should be given respect and honor as a person? Or do you see your spouse as an obstacle to the things that you desire or a shield that fails to protect you from the things you fear?

SOMETHING TO THINK ABOUT:

Whose best interests (yours? your spouses?) usually shape the way you think and feel about your spouse?

How might your typical pattern of relating sometimes reflect manipulation and at other times be a genuine expression of love?

Cultivating an Attitude of Honoring

Read Philippians 2:1–18 and then answer the questions.

> ¹If you have any encouragement from being united with Christ, if any comfort from his love, if any fellowship with the Spirit, if any tenderness and compassion, ²then make my joy complete by being like-minded, having the same love, being one in spirit and purpose. ³Do nothing out of selfish ambition or vain conceit, but in humility consider others better than yourselves. ⁴Each of you should look not only to your own interests, but also to the interests of others.
>
> ⁵Your attitude should be the same as that of Christ Jesus: ⁶Who, being in very nature God, did not consider equality

with God something to be grasped, ⁷but made himself nothing, taking the very nature of a servant, being made in human likeness. ⁸And being found in appearance as a man, he humbled himself and became obedient to death—even death on a cross! ⁹Therefore God exalted him to the highest place and gave him the name that is above every name, ¹⁰that at the name of Jesus every knee should bow, in heaven and on earth and under the earth, ¹¹and every tongue confess that Jesus Christ is Lord, to the glory of God the Father.

¹²Therefore, my dear friends, as you have always obeyed—not only in my presence, but now much more in my absence—continue to work out your salvation with fear and trembling, ¹³for it is God who works in you to will and to act according to his good purpose.

¹⁴Do everything without complaining or arguing, ¹⁵so that you may become blameless and pure, children of God without fault in a crooked and depraved generation, in which you shine like stars in the universe ¹⁶as you hold out the word of life—in order that I may boast on the day of Christ that I did not run or labor for nothing. ¹⁷But even if I am being poured out like a drink offering on the sacrifice and service coming from your faith, I am glad and rejoice with all of you. ¹⁸So you too should be glad and rejoice with me.

1. *List some of your spouse's strengths or abilities.*

2. *How might you learn from these strengths? How might God use them to help you grow? Can you see how your spouse's strengths are evidence of God's grace, things God wants to bless you with?*

3. *Think about some of the typical frustrations or "ordinary moments" of your marriage. How might God be asking you to learn and grow from those as well?*

BUILDING YOUR RELATIONSHIP WITH EACH OTHER

As a couple, read the following pages and complete all the activities and questions.

Read Philippians 2:1–18 together (passage is printed out above in the individual homework section).

Read the following examples and try to decide what is being demonstrated: manipulation or honoring. Hint: think about whose purpose is being served in each statement.

A. I need you. I don't think I could live without you.

B. I could really use your input on this. I'm just not sure what to do.

C. If you really loved me you'd be taking my side on this issue!

D. Don't ever embarrass me in front of my friends like that again!

E. Sometimes giving someone the cold shoulder is the best way to get their attention.

F. God, please help me to do what most pleases you and is best for my family.

G. I can learn things from my spouse.

Pray together using Philippians 2:1–18 as your guide. Ask God to help you fulfill his purpose for your marriage. Ask God to reveal to you ways that you manipulate rather than honor each other.

BEFORE THE NEXT SESSION:
In *Marriage Matters*, read Chapter 7 and the beginning of Chapter 8 (pages 93–116).

Unit 4

Communication: Honesty and Oneness

KEY PASSAGE: EPHESIANS 4:14–25

KEY IDEAS:

1. Honesty springs from oneness.
2. On the one hand, we want to be known and loved; on the other hand, we often avoid knowing ourselves and know that it isn't entirely safe to be known by another sinner.
3. Speaking the truth in love, we will become like Christ.
4. We can impart the grace and mercy that we ourselves have received from Christ.
5. Emotions play an important role in honesty. When we are able to share our emotions with our spouses we are more effective at expressing sincere love. Anger and fear are emotions that require extra care. Both can tempt us to cover rather than reveal ourselves.
6. True fellowship comes from being willing to walk in the light.

TO PREPARE FOR THIS SESSION:

In *Marriage Matters*, read Chapter 7 and the beginning of Chapter 8 (pages 93–116).

Lesson 4

OPENING

Share briefly something you learned from doing the homework this week.

Key Idea: Honesty springs from oneness.

How often have you complained that you and your spouse don't communicate? Often this complaint is not pointing to a failure of communication, instead it is pointing to a failure of honesty. People don't hear what their spouses mean to say, nor are they being completely honest about what they themselves are thinking. The apostle Paul writes, "Therefore each of you must put off falsehood and speak truthfully to his neighbor, for we are all members of one body" (Ephesians 4:25).

What two things must we do as a part of one body?

THE PROBLEM OF HIDING

Key Idea: On the one hand, we want to be known and loved; on the other hand, we often avoid knowing ourselves and know that it isn't entirely safe to be known by another sinner.

No matter how much you love and trust your spouse there are probably things that you don't want them to know about you. Before the Fall, Adam and Eve knew nothing of that feeling. There was nothing to hide or avoid.

Read the following verses from Genesis and discuss the questions.

²⁵The man and his wife were both naked, and they felt no shame.

¹Now the serpent was more crafty than any of the wild animals the LORD God had made. He said to the woman, "Did God really say, 'You must not eat from any tree in the garden'?" ²The woman said to the serpent, "We may eat fruit from the trees in the garden, ³but God did say, 'You must not eat fruit from the tree that is in the middle of the garden, and you must not touch it, or you will die.'"

⁴"You will not surely die," the serpent said to the woman. ⁵"For God knows that when you eat of it your eyes will be opened, and you will be like God, knowing good and evil."

⁶When the woman saw that the fruit of the tree was good for food and pleasing to the eye, and also desirable for gaining wisdom, she took some and ate it. She also gave some to her husband, who was with her, and he ate it. ⁷Then the eyes of both of them were opened, and they realized they were naked; so they sewed fig leaves together and made coverings for themselves. ⁸Then the man and his wife heard the sound of the LORD God as he was walking in the garden in the cool of the day, and they hid from the LORD God among the trees of the garden. ⁹But the LORD God called to the man, "Where are you?"

¹⁰He answered, "I heard you in the garden, and I was afraid because I was naked; so I hid."

¹¹And he said, "Who told you that you were naked? Have you eaten from the tree that I commanded you not to eat from?"

¹²The man said, "The woman you put here with me—she gave me some fruit from the tree, and I ate it."

¹³Then the LORD God said to the woman, "What is this you have done?"

The woman said, "The serpent deceived me, and I ate."
(Genesis 2:25—3:13)

1. What is the big change that occurs from Genesis 2:25 to Genesis 3:13?

2. What did Satan do to cause this fall?

3. What did Adam and Eve do that shows they began hiding from each other?

4. What did they do that shows they began hiding from God?

5. *What did they do that shows they began hiding from themselves?*

SOMETHING TO THINK ABOUT:

On the one hand we're wired to know and love God, and on the other, our sinfulness compels us to rail against him and avoid him. Thus we live as divided people, always of two minds. Sometimes we genuinely desire to draw near to God, to embrace him, to love him, and to love others. However, in the very next moment we can feel the complete opposite impulse. Wild desires seize us, animosity and anger flare up, and we inwardly shake our fists at God and others. The apostle Paul describes this internal warfare this way: "For I have the desire to do what is good, but I cannot carry it out. For what I do is not the good I want to do; no, the evil I do not want to do—this I keep on doing. Now if I do what I do not want to do, it is no longer I who do it, but it is sin living in me that does it" (Romans 7:18b–20).

This is the dynamic that shows up when we try to communicate in marriage. On the one hand we want to be known and loved. On the other hand, we often avoid knowing ourselves and know that it isn't entirely safe to be known by another sinner. We don't know what should be said and what should be left unsaid. We tell selective truths, sometimes hiding from our spouses the most important things that are going on inside of us.

SPEAKING TRUTH IN LOVE

Key Idea: Speaking the truth in love, we will become like Christ.

Read this passage and discuss the questions.

> [14]Then we will no longer be infants, tossed back and forth by the waves, and blown here and there by every wind of teaching and by the cunning and craftiness of men in their deceitful scheming. [15]Instead, speaking the truth in love, we will in all things grow up into him who is the Head, that is, Christ. [16]From him the whole body, joined and held together by every supporting ligament, grows and builds itself up in love, as each part does its work.
>
> [17]So I tell you this, and insist on it in the Lord, that you must no longer live as the Gentiles do, in the futility of their thinking. [18]They are darkened in their understanding and separated from the life of God because of the ignorance that is in them due to the hardening of their hearts. [19]Having lost all sensitivity, they have given themselves over to sensuality so as to indulge in every kind of impurity, with a continual lust for more.
>
> [20]You, however, did not come to know Christ that way. [21]Surely you heard of him and were taught in him in accordance with the truth that is in Jesus. [22]You were taught, with regard to your former way of life, to put off your old self, which is being corrupted by its deceitful desires; [23]to be made new in the attitude of your minds; [24]and to put on the new self, created to be like God in true righteousness and holiness.
>
> [25]Therefore each of you must put off falsehood and speak truthfully to his neighbor, for we are all members of one body. (Ephesians 4:14–25)

1. *Underline every word or phrase that has to do with lying or hiding.*

2. *Circle every word or phrase that has to do with honesty and openness.*

3. What is the result of speaking the truth in love?

4. Why do we speak the truth?

5. What are some evidences of a hardened heart?

SPEAKING WITH GRACE AND MERCY

Key Idea: We can impart the grace and mercy that we ourselves have received from Christ.

Read Hebrews 4:15–16 and discuss the questions.

> For we do not have a high priest who is unable to sympathize with our weaknesses, but we have one who has been tempted in every way, just as we are—yet was without sin.

Let us then approach the throne of grace with confidence, so that we may receive mercy and find grace to help us in our time of need.

1. *What allows us to go to Christ with our weaknesses and needs with confidence instead of with fear?*

2. *How should you imitate Christ's example with your spouse?*

3. *What can husbands and wives do practically to show these qualities to each other? (What do grace and mercy look and sound like? What does the opposite of grace and mercy look and sound like?)*

EMOTIONS: ANGER AND FEAR

Key Idea: Emotions play an important role in honesty. When we are able to share our emotions with our spouses we are more effective at expressing sincere love. Anger and fear are emotions that require extra care. Both can tempt us to cover rather than reveal ourselves.

Anger

Anger has a powerful psychological and physical appeal. Psychologically, anger typically orients us to the faults of others. It tells us that someone has treated us unfairly, injured us, or threatened something that is important to us. Anger invites us to expose our spouses while directing attention away from our own faults.

Anger has a powerful physical appeal also. You *feel* anger in your body. Anger infuses you with energy and prepares you for launching a counterattack.

Anger does not have to be the enemy of honesty. In fact, God's love drives his anger. Much human anger can be destructive and dangerous, but anger can accomplish good. A mother dashes into the street to pull her child out of the way of a car and then angrily scolds the tot. Her anger is motivated by genuine concern for her child. Similarly, God's anger is motivated by his love for his children. In loving anger he addresses our sin, warning, beseeching, and disciplining by bringing consequences to instruct us. Ultimately, he sent Jesus to pay the penalty for our sins. The cross of Christ is both an act of love and an act of anger. In love, God defeats the enemy, sin, and creates a way for us to be restored to relationship with him.

As you worship God, your anger can become more like his. You can use the energy of your anger to examine yourself, not just your spouse. If your anger is to be like God's anger, you must be angry at sin wherever you find it—especially in yourself. And once you've identified your own sin, turned from it, and received God's forgiveness, you can humbly and lovingly address the wrongs of others.

Discuss the following:

1. Describe a time when you've seen anger expressed in a godly, constructive way. (If you can't think of an actual event then imagine one.)

2. Describe a time when you regretted expressing anger and a time when you regretted **not** expressing anger.

3. Why do you think examining your own sin first is necessary to addressing wrongs in your spouse?

Fear

Focusing on what might happen next, fear makes you want to run, hide, cover up, and protect yourself. Given the fact that we all struggle with sin, we can assume that honesty and fear will often accompany each other. We know we need to be honest, but we're afraid to be. Our fear of honesty isn't entirely unfounded. When we tell our spouses how they have hurt or offended us, or when we confess how we've hurt and offended them, we give them power. With that information they have the power to attack us where we are vulnerable. If I say to my wife, "I was really hurt when you said that I should lose some weight," I run the risk of hearing her say it again. If she *wants* to hurt me she can use that information as a weapon and call me "fatty" or make snide comments at the dinner table. I have exposed myself to that possibility. Obviously, if my spouse has a track record of abusing my honesty then my fear informs me that I should be cautious in practicing honesty. In such instances the first order of business would be to talk about how previous honesty has been abused and how that is damaging to the marriage.

Often we fear honesty because as descendents of Adam we are born with a sense that if we are truly known we will be rejected and punished. That's when we need to connect with the simple truth of the gospel. God has loved us by revealing himself as our gracious and loving Savior. Because of this we now can love our spouses by revealing ourselves to them.

Discuss the following questions:

1. *When we run, cover up, and hide our true feelings from our spouses, what impact does that have on our marriage relationship?*

2. *What about knowing Christ might help us to risk sharing honestly with our spouses?*

3. *How can we make it safer for our spouses to share with us?*

4. *What do you do when you feel anger or fear? What does God want you to do?*

5. *List some things you know about God that can start to deliver you from the control of anger or fear.*

Homework for Unit 4

Key Idea: True fellowship comes from being willing to walk in the light.

Complete this homework before the next session. Record your thoughts and responses below and bring it to the group meeting.

BUILDING YOUR RELATIONSHIP WITH GOD

On your own, read the following and complete all the activities and questions.

Prayerfully reread Ephesians 4:14–25 (printed out in the "Speaking Truth in Love" section of the lesson).

Sharing Emotions

Because emotions are a part of who we are as God's image-bearers, they are critical to the meaningful expression of honesty and love.

Your emotions tell you—and, when you express them, they tell others—how important something is to you. The stronger the emotion, the more important it is to you. The absence of emotion doesn't communicate neutrality, logic, or intelligence; it communicates indifference.

There isn't one right way to experience and express emotions. Spouses with different backgrounds and personality traits will have different ways of expressing emotions. We shouldn't try to force our spouses to match our style or preferences, but we should make an effort to show love by letting them know we are sharing in their experiences.

Read Hebrews 4:12–16 and answer the questions that follow.

> [12]For the word of God is living and active. Sharper than any double-edged sword, it penetrates even to dividing soul and spirit, joints and marrow; it judges the thoughts and attitudes of the heart. [13]Nothing in all creation is hidden from

God's sight. Everything is uncovered and laid bare before the eyes of him to whom we must give account.

[14]Therefore, since we have a great high priest who has gone through the heavens, Jesus the Son of God, let us hold firmly to the faith we profess. [15]For we do not have a high priest who is unable to sympathize with our weaknesses, but we have one who has been tempted in every way, just as we are—yet was without sin. [16]Let us then approach the throne of grace with confidence, so that we may receive mercy and find grace to help us in our time of need.

1. *Do you tend to (a) evaluate and judge your spouse's emotions or (b) share and sympathize with them? If you're not sure, ask your spouse.*

2. *Do you use/share your emotions to foster intimacy or to hide your true faults?*

3. *Recall a recent event that made you feel angry or afraid. Consider it in light of the Hebrews passage and write a prayer telling God how you feel. Ask God to enable you to view this event in light of his all-knowing grace and kindness to you.*

BUILDING YOUR RELATIONSHIP WITH EACH OTHER

As a couple, read the following pages and complete all the activities and questions.

Read Ephesians 4:14–25 one more time, this time together.

Now that you have a better understanding of the role that emotions play in our relationships you can begin to practice sharing them with each other.

1. *Think of a childhood memory in which you were especially happy (for example, a Christmas memory, a birthday party, or special vacation with the family). Jot down everything you remember*

about that memory—sights, sounds, smells, tastes, conversations, etc. Include a description of how you felt at the time it happened and even now as you reflect on it.

2. *Taking turns, share those memories with each other, being careful to use words that describe your feelings, not just the details of the memory. As you listen to your spouse share their memory do your best to affirm their feelings and, as best you can, enter into their experience with them perhaps imagining what it would have been like to have shared that time with them.*

Reflect together on your experience of sharing these memories and feelings with each other. Was it difficult? Was it enjoyable? If the exercise went well you may repeat it exploring another emotion that is a bit more difficult to share. For example, think of a memory that made you feel anxious. It doesn't have to be the most intensely anxious moment of your life. Choose a memory that feels manageable, not one that might overwhelm you.

BEFORE THE NEXT SESSION:

In *Marriage Matters*, read Chapter 8 starting on page 116 and Chapter 9 (pages 116–135).

Unit 5

Constructive Communication

KEY PASSAGE: EPHESIANS 4:29

KEY IDEAS:

1. Our attempts at communication often backfire because rather than revealing our own thoughts and feelings we tell our spouses what we believe is wrong with them.
2. Dishonesty may mean we are trusting ourselves rather than God.
3. Honest communication does not mean saying the first thing that comes to mind. The goal is always to speak the truth in love with the purpose of building up the other.
4. Honesty that builds relationship affirms God's love for our spouses, is based on a careful understanding of them, and is sensitive to the timing of our words.

TO PREPARE FOR THIS SESSION:

In *Marriage Matters*, read Chapter 8 starting on page 116 and Chapter 9 (pages 116–135).

Lesson 5

OPENING

Key Idea: Our attempts at communication often backfire because rather than revealing our own thoughts and feelings we tell our spouses what we believe is wrong with them.

- *Share something you learned from the homework.*

- *List a few reasons why honesty can be difficult in marriage.*

- *What role do you think our emotions might play in practicing honesty and oneness?*

COMMON FORMS OF DISHONESTY

Key Idea: Dishonesty may mean we are trusting ourselves rather than God.

One of the common ways we experience our sinfulness is a desire to somehow cover ourselves and hide (Genesis 3:7–9). Dishonesty is one of the ways we trust in ourselves and "hide" rather than trusting in God and loving our spouses by being honest. Sometimes we outright lie to our spouses, but much of the dishonesty that cripples communication is subtle, of a kind that you might not notice or even recognize as dishonesty. Three common forms of dishonesty are the double bind, indirection, and misdirection.

In a *double bind*, truth is joined to a contradictory message that makes it almost impossible for a spouse to know how to respond. No matter which message they respond to, they lose. A tone of voice, facial expression, or body language contradicts the words being spoken.

Indirection occurs when, to soften the truth, casual hints are dropped. Potentially offensive messages are delivered in offhand comments. This technique gives the speaker wiggle room to deny that the offensive message was the one intended.

Misdirection occurs when, instead of broaching a difficult topic, a counterfeit problem is manufactured.

Read the following scenarios and,

    A. Decide what form dishonesty takes in each.
    B. Discuss how each form of dishonesty employs selfishness and self-protection.
    C. Describe how the person being dishonest is refusing to trust Jesus.

Scenario 1

Sexual intimacy is very important to Barry, but he is reluctant to talk about it with his wife, Janine. Barry has been growing increasingly upset, feeling there hasn't been frequent or regular sexual intimacy. Janine has shown little interest, he thinks, and he feels rejected and separated from his wife. Yet discussing the issue openly and honestly with his wife seems too risky. As his frustration builds he finds it more and more difficult to conceal it, but he would rather talk about anything else than let his wife know that he misses her.

Instead, he vents his frustration and anger on anything and everything that seems to stand between him and his wife's affections: "I don't understand why you have to hold our kids' hands the whole time they're doing their homework! They have to learn to do it on their own! You aren't going to go to college with them are you?" "I'm tired of the phone constantly interrupting our evenings! We need uninterrupted family time. No more phone calls after 7 p.m.!"

The real issue is never put on the table. Venting anger may bring some temporary relief for the husband, but his wife is certainly no closer to understanding what is really bothering him, and she is no more romantically inclined after being attacked for what normally goes unnoticed.

Scenario 2

Bernice wishes that her husband were more helpful around the house but has found that asking for his help only irritates him. So she looks for opportunities to get the message across other ways. She knows that he really values having time with her in the evenings so she goes to bed an hour or two early for a few nights making sure to explain to her husband that she's just too tired from all of the housework to stay awake another minute. (Hint: If you would just help me, I'd be more available to spend time with you!) How should the husband respond? Even if he takes the hint, it's hard for him to respond well. His wife isn't being honest and he feels manipulated. If he takes offense and angrily responds, "I know, you're trying to tell me I need to do more to help out around here," his wife can deny that she was trying to send a message at all and tell her husband he's too sensitive and overreacting.

Scenario 3

One form of dishonesty that I have come to recognize in myself is pouting. Pouting is just what you think it is—a look of sadness or irritation accompanied by silence and withdrawal. It works this way: my wife, Kim, does something that angers me or hurts my feelings. Rather than speak honestly about it, I become sullen and withdraw.

If she asks me what's wrong, I say, "Nothing." But my tone, facial expression, and body language all scream, "Everything!" What is she to do? If she listens to my body language and challenges my words then I become increasingly angry with her for doubting me. If she listens to my words and ignores my body language the pouting intensifies while I smolder on the inside thinking, "She really doesn't care! If she cared, she would be asking me what's wrong!"

1. *Have you ever used one of these forms of dishonesty?*

2. *What can you do to make sure you are speaking honestly to your spouse?*

3. *How do you think trusting Christ will help you to communicate honestly with your spouse?*

COMMON WAYS TO DISTORT THE TRUTH

Key Idea: Honest communication does not mean saying the first thing that comes to mind. The goal is always to speak the truth in love with the purpose of building up the other.

Read the following verse and discuss the questions:

> Do not let any unwholesome talk come out of your mouths, but only what is helpful for building others up according to their needs, that it may benefit those who listen. (Ephesians 4:29)

1. *According to this verse, what should never come out of our mouths?*

2. *How can we know if something we say is unwholesome?*

3. *How does this affect how we "tell the truth"?*

SOMETHING TO THINK ABOUT:

The wise person understands how powerful words can be and uses them carefully. Constructive honesty requires us to know the difference between what we think or feel and what we should share. Wisdom also means that we know our spouse well enough to decide what should be shared, how to share it, and when to share it or when to just keep our thoughts to ourselves.

There are some kinds of honest expression that are loaded with corrosive content.

1. Exaggeration—Using absolute terms like *only*, *always*, and *never*.

Imagine your spouse has said some harsh things to you. After a few minutes he or she cools off and tries to apologize. At this point you say, "You know, it would help if you weren't so critical *all* the time! You *never* say anything nice to me!" How would your spouse respond? By becoming defensive, right? Is your spouse still ready to apologize?

You were right to say how hurtful the angry criticism was, but the truth was distorted by offensive exaggerations. Consider how different it would have been if you had said, "You know it really hurts me when you lose your temper like that. And sometimes I feel like you are disappointed with me more often than you are happy with me." It might have deepened your spouse's understanding of what happened, which would have deepened his or her apology rather than negating it.

2. Using trait names—reducing the other's identity to his or her sinful behavior.

Sometimes in a heated argument, spouses say things that are especially destructive. Instead of saying, "I feel like you weren't being honest with me," they say "You're a liar." Instead of saying, "You really hurt me when you said…" they say "You're a jerk!"

Trait names reduce a spouse's identity to his or her sinful behavior. Like exaggeration, using trait names communicates, "You are no more and no better than what you've just done."

3. Mind reading—assuming the worst.

Bill and Mary had a real blowout and said some very ugly things. Sometime later Bill came home with a dozen roses, planted a passionate kiss on Mary, and announced that he had arranged for a babysitter and that they were going out to Mary's favorite restaurant. Mary angrily pushed Bill away and proclaimed, "Don't think I don't know what you're up to! You want me to just forget all the mean things that you said by sweeping me off my feet, buying me dinner, and even expecting me to have sex with you tonight! Well, you can just forget it!"

Mary acts as if she can read Bill's mind; as if she not only knows what Bill is doing, but why he's doing it. Is Mary right about Bill? It is true that surprises and gifts have become Bill's regular response to fights, and that the gifts have the effect of burying the conflict rather than resolving it. But does that mean Bill is being manipulative? Does that mean he's just after sex? Maybe, but it could also be that Bill simply doesn't know of any other way to recover. Maybe he doesn't know how to solve the problem and is afraid to engage in it again. The point is, we don't know.

4. Shaming.

At one point during a counseling session with a couple, the wife became so angry and desperate for me to side with her against her husband that she blurted out, "You don't understand how sick he is! Did I tell you what he did in college?!"

Her husband jerked his head around and stared wide-eyed at her. Before she could say another word I held up my hands and said, "Stop! Don't say another word!" I couldn't have been more emphatic or determined to stop her if she had pulled the pin on a hand grenade and threatened to throw it at him. I don't know what she was going to say, but I do know that if she had said it, marriage counseling, and possibly the marriage itself, would be over. Her husband would have been humiliated, and likely enraged, by whatever she was going to share.

One of the biggest challenges to honesty is shame, our sense that there are things about us that make us unacceptable and unlovable, things that we feel we must hide. Marriage gives us an opportunity both to give and to receive the same kind of love that God gives us, a love that communicates that we can be known and loved. It is especially egregious, then, when in a moment of anger a spouse takes something you've shared in a moment of intimacy and safety and uses it as a weapon against you. When you shame your spouse in this way, you are not only humiliating your spouse and breaking trust; you are actively attacking the work of the gospel in his or her life. Where God says, "You are forgiven," you are saying, "You will always be guilty." Where the gospel says, "You are now clean," you say, "You are still filthy." When you shame your spouse you aren't just offending your spouse, but God himself.

1. What do all of these ways we distort truth have in common?

2. Why don't these distortions of truth ever work?

Read the following scenario and identify the distortions of truth being used.

"Stephanie, we're all in the car! We've been waiting for you for 10 minutes and now we're late! Can you please hurry it up?!"

"I thought you said we needed to be there at 5? It's only 4:30; we have plenty of time!"

"You always do this and make everyone late. You know I hate being late, but all you care about is yourself. Just pick out something to wear and wear it."

"Scott, I would have been down already if you had gotten the kids ready like I asked you too. But like always you were probably watching TV. If we're late it'll be because of you—don't blame me. You're lazy! Show some patience for once in your life!"

"I will not be patient! Do you remember what happened last time you made us late? And whose fault was that?!"

SOMETHING TO THINK ABOUT:

Do any of these distortions of truth appear in your speech with your spouse? Are you willing to give your spouse permission to point out any of these distortions and will you accept responsibility by confessing to the distortion and re-speaking your words?

Homework for Unit 5

Key Idea: Honesty that builds relationship affirms God's love for our spouses, is based on a careful understanding of them, and is sensitive to the timing of our words.

Complete this homework before the next session. Record your thoughts and responses below and bring it to the group meeting.

BUILDING YOUR RELATIONSHIP WITH GOD

On your own, read the following pages and complete all the activities and questions.

In the book of Ephesians, before Paul tells his readers to live a life worthy of their calling (Ephesians 4:1), he reminds them in chapters 1–3 of who they really are and what they have in Christ.

1. *Read Ephesians 1–3. Who are you and what do you have in Christ?*

2. *How can remembering who you and your spouse are in Christ help you communicate truth in love?*

3. *Identify two or three strengths your spouse has that could be used in a positive way in your communication with each other.*

4. List some things you want to work on in your communication with your spouse.

Remembering who you are in Christ may be a positive way to begin those difficult conversations. How different would difficult conversations be if they were punctuated with some of the following attitudes and statements?

- "**I know God wants better for us. Let's take some time to cool off and pray.**" Bring God into the discussion, not to come across as spiritually superior, but to remember that he is as real a part of your marriage and your problems as anyone.
- "**Even if we disagree, let's assume God has something to teach both of us**." Remember that God intends to work through our marriages to help us to grow. Even in conflict, speak to one another in a way that communicates a willingness to learn and grow.
- "**One of the things I've always loved about you is your (Fill in the blank with whatever fits your spouse and the situation). We don't have to hide from this problem**." How can you draw on the strengths that each of you brought to the marriage? This is a way of remembering and recognizing that God has given us gifts to strengthen and bless each other.

If you remember from Hebrews 4:15–16, because Christ stepped into our world and sympathizes with our weaknesses, we can approach him with confidence. God's love is "incarnational."

That means that God hasn't loved us from afar, but in Jesus he has visited our world, experienced what we experience, and faced what we face.

Our marriages require that same process. We need to visit each other's world with the intention of truly understanding each other. Here are a few basic ingredients to being incarnational:

- **Let your spouse know that you want to understand**. Ask questions to which you truly want an answer without assuming you already know it. Be humble enough to be willing to hear something new and learn from it.
- **Check out your understanding**. Put what you think you're hearing into your own words and see if your spouse agrees with you. Do this as many times as you need to until your spouse agrees that you understand. You don't have to agree with what your spouse is saying, but your spouse does need to know that you at least understand what he or she is trying to say. There is no point in moving on to the next idea or speaking to what you've heard if your spouse doesn't believe you understand what has already been said.
- **Emotionally respond to what you hear**. Your spouse needs to know that you are affected by what he or she has shared. That doesn't mean generating phony emotions. Just be honest about what you do feel. If you feel uncertain about what you've heard then share that. If you need more time to process it, share that. But your spouse needs to know that you care about what is important to him or her.

Timing

One of the results of knowing and understanding your spouse is developing a sense of timing. Speaking the truth in love isn't just about word choices, but also about the where and when you choose to speak. Having the right thing to say at the right place and at the right time brings joy to the one who gives it and the one who receives it. Take the time to find out the kind of truth your spouse needs *when* he or she needs it. When do they need encouragement?

When do they need advice? When do they simply need some time to think things through on their own before talking about it? If you aren't certain, ask!

Think of ways you can honestly affirm God's love for your spouse. Where do you see God's goodness reflected in their character or how they're growing as a person? How can you communicate this to them?

BUILDING YOUR RELATIONSHIP WITH EACH OTHER

As a couple, complete the following activities and questions.

Go somewhere where you can have a conversation. Use a few of the following questions as starting points.

- How is your relationship with God? What has been good? What do you feel you should improve?
- How do you picture our lives ten years from now?
- What do you feel would be the greatest thing you would still want to accomplish in your life?
- What sin has a tendency to still have control over you the most?
- What could I do to help you feel safe to share your thoughts with me?
- Is there anything else you feel you should share with me?
- Share your list of things you want to work on in communicating with your spouse. What fears may be obstacles to this process? What can you do to help eliminate the fears of your spouse?

BEFORE THE NEXT SESSION:

In *Marriage Matters*, read Chapters 10 and 11 (pages 137–162).

Unit 6

Conflict: God Is Up to Something Good

KEY PASSAGE: 1 CORINTHIANS 8:1

KEY IDEAS:
1. Conflicts are often battles for things we want.
2. Know your real enemy.
3. In conflict we are tempted to immediately place blame on our spouses, but the Bible teaches us to examine our own hearts and look for desires that we need to repent of because they have become more important to us than loving God or our spouse.
4. Decide which approach to use in conflict (yield, wait, or confront) by discerning which one will best serve the needs of your spouse.
5. Working through conflict in a godly way requires that you grow in wisdom and act in love. You need the wisdom to size up your own heart, your spouse's heart, and the situation as best you can, and to act in faith and love.
6. The Bible tells us that conflict does not have to be destructive. In fact, God promises to use conflict to expose and eradicate sin and help us to grow in love.

TO PREPARE FOR THIS SESSION:
In *Marriage Matters*, read Chapters 10 and 11 (pages 137–162).

Lesson 6

OPENING

Key Idea: Conflicts are often battles for things we want.

Read or act out the following skit. Then, briefly discuss the causes of the conflict between Jack and Michelle.

>   JACK sits at the kitchen table paying some bills, when MICHELLE bursts into the room.
>   MICHELLE: Do you think it is too much to ask for a little help putting the kids to bed! Couldn't you hear the grief they were giving me!
>   JACK: It sounded like you had everything under control.
>   MICHELLE: I'm just saying it would be nice to have a little help from you once in a while.
>   JACK: I help! What do you think I'm doing? I'll gladly let *you* pay the bills and *I'll* put the kids to bed next time! It isn't that difficult.
>   MICHELLE: You never listen to me! *(Michelle storms away.)*
>   JACK: *(yelling)* I am listening! You're just not making any sense!

THE NATURE OF CONFLICT

Key Idea: Know your real enemy.

Read the following passages and answer the questions.

>   [10]Finally, be strong in the Lord and in his mighty power. [11]Put on the full armor of God so that you can take your stand against the devil's schemes. [12]For our struggle is not against flesh and blood, but against the rulers, against the authorities, against the powers of this dark world and against the spiritual forces of evil in the heavenly realms.

¹³Therefore put on the full armor of God, so that when the day of evil comes, you may be able to stand your ground, and after you have done everything, to stand. ¹⁴Stand firm then, with the belt of truth buckled around your waist, with the breastplate of righteousness in place, ¹⁵and with your feet fitted with the readiness that comes from the gospel of peace. ¹⁶In addition to all this, take up the shield of faith, with which you can extinguish all the flaming arrows of the evil one. ¹⁷Take the helmet of salvation and the sword of the Spirit, which is the word of God. ¹⁸And pray in the Spirit on all occasions with all kinds of prayers and requests. With this in mind, be alert and always keep on praying for all the saints. (Ephesians 6:10–18)

¹What causes fights and quarrels among you? Don't they come from your desires that battle within you? ²You want something but don't get it. You kill and covet, but you cannot have what you want. You quarrel and fight. (James 4:1–2a)

¹"Do not judge, or you too will be judged. ²For in the same way you judge others, you will be judged, and with the measure you use, it will be measured to you.
³"Why do you look at the speck of sawdust in your brother's eye and pay no attention to the plank in your own eye? ⁴How can you say to your brother, 'Let me take the speck out of your eye,' when all the time there is a plank in your own eye? ⁵You hypocrite, first take the plank out of your own eye, and then you will see clearly to remove the speck from your brother's eye." (Matthew 7:1–5)

1. *What is the source of our quarrels and conflicts?*

2. *Against who or what do we struggle?*

3. *According to Ephesians 6 what should be our protection?*

4. *If quarrels, as James says, come from the desires within us, where should we begin to bring a positive outcome out of conflict?*

5. *What keeps us from first examining our own hearts?*

6. *What could help you in the midst of conflict to be ready and willing to first "take the plank out of your own eye"?*

HOW DO WE EXAMINE OUR OWN HEARTS?

Key Idea: In conflict we are tempted to immediately place blame on our spouses, but the Bible teaches us to examine our own hearts and look for desires that we need to repent of because they have become more important to us than loving God or our spouse.

If quarrels are caused by the desires within us, we should first identify those desires. The question "What do you want?" is different from "What are you fighting *about*?" What you are fighting about is the set of circumstances that precipitated the conflict. What you want concerns the real *issues* that drive the conflict. The Bible challenges us to dig beneath the details of the event, and uncover deeper issues of the heart.

1. *Back to Jack and Michelle: what do you think are the real issues that drive their conflict?*

2. How could Michelle have rephrased her complaints to Jack?

3. What could be some wrong motives for being willing to examine your own heart first?

4. When we think of conflict, we sometimes think in terms of a winner and a loser, a stronger and a weaker. How is godly conflict different?

5. *How do you think being the first to ask God and your spouse for forgiveness might change a marriage conflict? What are some reasons we might be unwilling to do that?*

A BIBLICAL APPROACH TO CONFLICT

Key Idea: Decide which approach to use in conflict (yield, wait, or confront) by discerning which one will best serve the needs of your spouse.

Left to our own devices, we handle conflict in one of three ways: we appease, we ignore, or we win. When we appease, we look for a way to satisfy the other so there is no reason for conflict. When we ignore, we pretend the problem doesn't exist. When we win, problems are settled because we defeat the other party through persuasion and intimidation.

All three of these methods are flawed and easily corrupted by the deceitful desires and fears of our heart.

The question is: What does *love* look like in conflict? Let's examine some Scripture verses that can help us to construct a godly strategy governed by love.

Read the Scripture verses in the left column and in the right column make a note of how those verses say that conflict should be handled.

Scripture	How to Handle Conflict
Starting a quarrel is like breaching a dam; so drop the matter before a dispute breaks out. (Prov. 17:14)	
It is to a man's honor to avoid strife, but every fool is quick to quarrel. (Prov. 20:3)	
Do not hate your brother in your heart. Rebuke your neighbor frankly so you will not share in his guilt. Do not seek revenge or bear a grudge against one of your people, but love your neighbor as yourself. I am the Lord. (Lev. 19:17–18)	
"If your brother sins against you, go and show him his fault, just between the two of you. If he listens to you, you have won your brother over. But if he will not listen, take one or two others along, so that 'every matter may be established by the testimony of two or three witnesses.'" (Matt. 18:15–16)	
If it is possible, as far as it depends on you, live at peace with everyone. (Rom. 12:18)	
But the wisdom that comes from heaven is first of all pure; then peace-loving, considerate, submissive, full of mercy and good fruit, impartial and sincere. Peacemakers who sow in peace raise a harvest of righteousness. (James 3:17–18)	
Make every effort to live in peace with all men. (Heb. 12:14)	

Everything in the right column can be grouped into three categories: yielding, waiting, or confronting. Notice that these three biblical ways to respond to conflict are similar to the appeasing, ignoring, and winning strategies.

The Bible gives us more than one strategy because different people and situations require different approaches. How do you know which one to use? Since our foundation is God's love, ask yourself which approach would most benefit the other. Answering that question requires more than a technical understanding of one approach or another, it requires you to know yourself and your spouse.

THE KEY: LOVE IS MORE THAN RIGHT AND WRONG

Key Idea: Working through conflict in a godly way requires that you grow in wisdom and act in love. You need the wisdom to size up your own heart, your spouse's heart, and the situation as best you can, and to act in faith and love.

Read the following passage and answer the questions:

> ¹Now about food sacrificed to idols: We know that we all possess knowledge. Knowledge puffs up, but love builds up. ²The man who thinks he knows something does not yet know as he ought to know. ³But the man who loves God is known by God.
>
> ⁴So then, about eating food sacrificed to idols: We know that an idol is nothing at all in the world and that there is no God but one. ⁵For even if there are so-called gods, whether in heaven or on earth (as indeed there are many "gods" and many "lords"), ⁶yet for us there is but one God, the Father, from whom all things came and for whom we live; and there is but one Lord, Jesus Christ, through whom all things came and through whom we live.
>
> ⁷But not everyone knows this. Some people are still so accustomed to idols that when they eat such food they think

of it as having been sacrificed to an idol, and since their conscience is weak, it is defiled. ⁸But food does not bring us near to God; we are no worse if we do not eat, and no better if we do.

⁹Be careful, however, that the exercise of your freedom does not become a stumbling block to the weak. ¹⁰For if anyone with a weak conscience sees you who have this knowledge eating in an idol's temple, won't he be emboldened to eat what has been sacrificed to idols? ¹¹So this weak brother, for whom Christ died, is destroyed by your knowledge. ¹²When you sin against your brothers in this way and wound their weak conscience, you sin against Christ. ¹³Therefore, if what I eat causes my brother to fall into sin, I will never eat meat again, so that I will not cause him to fall. (1 Corinthians 8:1–13)

1. *What do you think the apostle Paul was trying to teach the Corinthians when he wrote "knowledge puffs up, but love builds up" (vs. 1)?*

2. *According to Paul, what is the correct answer to whether Christians could eat meat that had been sacrificed to idols?*

3. *What is the condition Paul places on this "right" to eat the meat? What do the Corinthians need to "be careful" of?*

4. *Which approach to handling conflict should you use?*

SOMETHING TO THINK ABOUT:

Real peace is more than the absence of conflict; it is a fruit of the Holy Spirit that is cultivated only by the eradication of sin and usually through conflict. We must then take seriously the Bible's call to do battle against sin where we find it—in our hearts and in our relationships. This means identifying the real enemy—not our spouse, but our sin. When spouses learn the difference between attacking each other and attacking sin, conflict takes on a whole new meaning.

Learning to work through conflict in a godly, constructive way will always be more than following a prescribed set of steps. It requires that you grow in wisdom and act in love. You need the wisdom to size up your own heart, your spouse's heart, and the situation as best you can, and to act in faith and love.

Homework for Unit 6

Key Idea: The Bible tells us that conflict does not have to be destructive. In fact, God promises to use conflict to expose and eradicate sin and help us to grow in love.

Complete this homework before the next session. Record your thoughts and responses below and bring it to the group meeting.

BUILDING YOUR RELATIONSHIP WITH GOD

On your own, complete these activities and questions.

We learned in the lesson that people have a natural tendency to handle conflict in one of three ways: by appeasing, ignoring, or winning.

1. *Which of these strategies do you tend to use?*

2. *Why do you think you handle conflict this way?*

3. *What connection if any do you see between your style of resolving conflict and the inner desires you identified in Unit 2?*

4. *Which biblical approach is most difficult for you: yielding, waiting, or confronting? Why?*

5. *Write about a recent conflict with your spouse. Include details about how you handled it. Think about how God would have wanted you to handle it.*

6. *Read James 4:6–10. Remember that God doesn't expect us to do any of these things in our own strength. But he can work through us—he can love through us and he can dispense grace through us.*

> ⁶But he gives us more grace. That is why Scripture says: "God opposes the proud but gives grace to the humble." ⁷Submit yourselves, then, to God. Resist the devil, and he will flee from you. ⁸Come near to God and he will come near to you. Wash your hands, you sinners, and purify your hearts, you double-minded. ⁹Grieve, mourn and wail. Change your laughter to mourning and your joy to gloom. ¹⁰Humble yourselves before the Lord, and he will lift you up.

Write a brief but specific prayer repenting if you need to, thanking God for the love and help he offers freely in Jesus, and asking for something particular in the way you handle conflict.

BUILDING YOUR RELATIONSHIP WITH EACH OTHER

As a couple, complete the following activities and questions.

Moments of marital conflict can be some of the most discouraging and destructive moments of all. Because the Bible teaches that peace is a hallmark of the Christian who's following Jesus, conflict can be doubly discouraging for Christians. Not only do we live in the marital wreckage it creates, but we feel like spiritual failures as well. Conflict can leave us feeling that we haven't only failed as husbands and wives but as Christians.

But the Bible also teaches that conflict may be a sign that God is at work. It isn't inherently wrong, a sign of failure, or evidence that God has somehow abandoned you or your marriage. In fact, from the very beginning God planned to use conflict to accomplish good in the lives of his people by destroying sin and establishing the very peace he desires.

Read all of Genesis 3 together paying special attention to verse 15: "I will put enmity between you and the woman, and between your offspring and hers; he will crush your head, and you will strike his heel."

1. *Who is God addressing in verse 15? What is his message to him?*

2. *Try to explain why verse 15 is sometimes referred to as the very first proclamation of the gospel.*

The conflict mentioned in verse 15 is going to be an epic battle that spans millennia; it is a battle between two offspring, Satan's and Eve's. Not only did God spare Adam and Eve, he also made a way for us, their offspring, to be a part of the solution. Although Satan desires to use conflict for his purposes, God has overruled his plans and claimed conflict for himself. God has taken the conflict that Satan started and turned it against him. Notice that God "places enmity" between Satan's offspring and Eve's offspring.

Jesus is the offspring promised in Genesis 3:15. In Christ, the great conflict that started in the beginning reaches a climax. He crushes the serpent's head, even as he is wounded—"struck in the heel"—on the cross. Jesus is wounded on the cross for our sins, but it is Satan who receives the fatal blow. By forgiving our sins and giving us new hearts, Jesus makes it possible for us to join God's family and grow and mature to be like him. As God's children through Jesus, we have the freedom to say no to sin and yes to God. That's where the battle continues for us. Jesus landed the fatal blow, but we have to join the battle to see it fulfilled in our lives and our marriages.

3. *How might understanding that God intends to use your conflicts for good purposes change your attitude toward conflict?*

4. *If Satan is the real enemy in conflict, what should your attitude toward your spouse be in the midst of it?*

KEY IDEAS TO HELP YOU WITH CONFLICT:

- Remember the big picture of conflict and don't give in to discouragement.
- Be alert to the dangers of defensiveness.
- Deal with your own sin first.
- Adopt the biblical approach that fits your knowledge of yourself, your spouse, and the need of the moment.
- Don't get stuck on who's right and who's wrong; always act to build up the other in love.

BEFORE THE NEXT SESSION:

In *Marriage Matters*, read Chapters 12 and 13 (pages 163–191).

Unit 7

Forgiveness

KEY PASSAGE: COLOSSIANS 3:13

KEY IDEAS:
1. While forgiveness is something that people do and can be observed, it is ultimately a supernatural act.
2. Learning to forgive as God forgives requires decisions to release, sacrifice, trust, and grow.
3. In forgiveness we practice and extend to others what God has given us.
4. To facilitate forgiveness in marriage focus on how your spouse has blessed you, how much you've been forgiven, and how you are subject to the same temptations and weaknesses.

TO PREPARE FOR THIS SESSION:
In *Marriage Matters,* read Chapters 12 and 13 (pages 163–191).

Lesson 7

OPENING
What do you know about forgiveness? Write T (true), F (false), or ? (I don't know) next to each statement.
1. Not everyone deserves to be forgiven.
2. There is a limit to what can be forgiven.

3. Forgiveness requires the other person to ask for forgiveness.
4. We should always forgive because God in Christ has forgiven us.
5. Forgiving someone removes all consequences.
6. Forgiving someone means letting go of your right to punish him.
7. Forgiveness does not always look the same for each person.
8. The purpose of forgiveness is to restore a relationship.
9. Forgiveness restores a relationship to where it once was.
10. Forgiveness has to flow from your emotions.
11. To truly forgive is to forget what happened.
12. Having to forgive someone is an unfortunate necessity.

FORGIVENESS DEFINED

Key Idea: While forgiveness is something that people do and can be observed, it is ultimately a supernatural act.

Read the passages and discuss the questions that follow.

> Therefore, if you are offering your gift at the altar and there remember that your brother has something against you, leave your gift there in front of the altar. First go and be reconciled to your brother; then come and offer your gift. (Matthew 5:23–24)

1. *What does this command reveal about what is important to God?*

2. *Why do you think this is important to God? (Think back to UNIT 1.)*

3. *What does this highlight about our worship of God and the act of forgiveness?*

⁵⁰And when Jesus had cried out again in a loud voice, he gave up his spirit. ⁵¹At that moment the curtain of the temple was torn in two from top to bottom. The earth shook and the rocks split. ⁵²The tombs broke open and the bodies of many holy people who had died were raised to life. (Matthew 27:50–52)

¹⁹Therefore, brothers, since we have confidence to enter the Most Holy Place by the blood of Jesus, ²⁰by a new and living way opened for us through the curtain, that is, his body, ²¹and since we have a great priest over the house of God, ²²let us draw near to God with a sincere heart in full assurance of faith, having our hearts sprinkled to cleanse us form a guilty conscience and having our bodies washed with pure water. (Hebrews 10:19–22)

4. *What images of God's forgiveness can you find in this passage?*

5. *How were these images reminders to the people of God's holiness and their sinfulness?*

6. *How were these images also reminders to the people of God's love for them?*

7. *What then was signified when the curtain was torn in two at Jesus' death?*

8. What do you think is the significance of the dead rising from their graves?

9. What has Jesus' death accomplished?

LEARNING TO FORGIVE AS GOD FORGIVES

Key Idea: Learning to forgive as God forgives requires decisions to release, sacrifice, trust, and grow.

> Bear with each other and forgive whatever grievances you may have against one another. Forgive as the Lord forgave you. (Colossians 3:13)

Embracing what Jesus has done for us and extending that in thought, word, and deed to others is the essence of forgiveness. In forgiving one another we, in a sense, draw on the forgiveness that Jesus has given us by making a decision to release another from the penalty of sin. Rather than drawing a curtain and pushing each other away, we push sin and judgment away and draw near to each other. Put as simply as possible, forgiveness is releasing the other from the penalty of sin so the relationship can be restored.

We are called to *do* something when we forgive and it is important to have practical steps in mind as you learn to forgive your spouse as God has forgiven you.

God decided to release us from the penalty of our sin.

God's forgiveness is based on the fact that Jesus paid our penalty. Our sin is removed as far as the east is from the west (Psalm 103:12). Because we ourselves have been forgiven, we can extend forgiveness to the one who has wronged us. Sticking to that decision requires us to refuse to dwell on how we've been wronged or bring it to mind. That means, for example, no subtle digs and not using it as a trump card in the next argument.

God decided to sacrifice in order to forgive.

God decided to absorb the cost of our sin. Repairing the relationship means accepting the wound and choosing to draw near to the one who has sought to harm him. God doesn't seek revenge or look for opportunities to pay us back for our sin. Likewise, we have to choose to draw near to our spouse without the lingering threat of some form of payback. We too will need to be willing to absorb the cost, facing the pain of the offense and the discomfort of talking about it.

God decided to accomplish good through our sinfulness.

God doesn't just forgive our sins, but promises to use even our messes for good. When we forgive our spouses, we have to trust that God will work for our good and the good of our marriage. Forgiveness becomes an opportunity to reflect the image of Christ and to mature in our faith. You have to trust that God will both heal your hurts and use your sacrifice to restore your relationship. When you forgive you have to trust that you are not being a fool, but that God will work through your forgiveness. Your forgiveness does not guarantee a change in your spouse, but it does guarantee that you will grow and that you will be protected from bitterness. Trust that forgiveness is the path that God provides to draw back the curtains that separate you and your spouse.

God decided to allow us to grow.

God's forgiveness is ongoing because we, of course, continue to sin. When we forgive our spouses, we can't expect perfection from them, but have to be willing to let them grow. And we have to understand that even our own ability to forgive will have to grow.

It's best not to think of these as sequential steps, but as different aspects of forgiveness. In the process of forgiveness there will be times when you will need to focus on one aspect more than others and you will likely have to revisit each aspect numerous times.

HOW FORGIVENESS WORKS

Key Idea: In forgiveness we practice and extend to others what God has given us.

Read the following scenario and determine what Jonathan will need to do to forgive his wife.

> After the church service, Jonathan was talking to Robert about the upcoming holiday. The conversation was light and amusing until Robert said, "I guess it may feel a little awkward if you're back at your in-laws this year."
> "What do you mean?" asked Jonathan.
> "Oh, well my wife mentioned how you said some things that maybe you wish you hadn't last time you were there."
> Jonathan felt like he had just been betrayed and sentenced all at the same time. How could his wife have talked to Robert's wife about that, especially since he had very clearly expressed his embarrassment and asked her to not talk about it with anyone. Jonathan felt hurt and angry.

1. How might Jonathan feel tempted to punish his wife?

2. What will it look like to release her from any penalty?

3. What might he need to sacrifice to be able to release her?

4. How can he set his mind to trust God and allow for growth?

5. *Are there aspects of forgiveness that are easier or harder for you than others? How would you explain the differences?*

6. *Go back to the questions at the beginning of this lesson and review your original answers. What questions do you still have about forgiveness?*

Homework for Unit 7

Key Idea: To facilitate forgiveness in marriage focus on how your spouse has blessed you, how much you've been forgiven, and how you are subject to the same temptations and weaknesses.

Complete this homework before the next session. Record your thoughts and responses below and bring it to the group meeting.

BUILDING YOUR RELATIONSHIP WITH GOD

On your own, complete these activities and questions.

Read Psalm 51 and answer the questions.

(A psalm of David. When the prophet Nathan came to him after David had committed adultery with Bathsheba.)
¹Have mercy on me, O God, according to your unfailing love; according to your great compassion blot out my transgressions. ²Wash away all my iniquity and cleanse me from my sin.

³For I know my transgressions, and my sin is always before me. ⁴Against you, you only, have I sinned and done what is evil in your sight, so that you are proved right when you speak and justified when you judge. ⁵Surely I was sinful at birth, sinful from the time my mother conceived me. ⁶Surely you desire truth in the inner parts; you teach me wisdom in the inmost place.

⁷Cleanse me with hyssop, and I will be clean; wash me, and I will be whiter than snow. ⁸Let me hear joy and gladness; let the bones you have crushed rejoice. ⁹Hide your face from my sins and blot out all my iniquity. ¹⁰Create in me a pure heart, O God, and renew a steadfast spirit within me. ¹¹Do not cast me from your presence or take your Holy Spirit from me. ¹²Restore to me the joy of your salvation and grant me a willing spirit, to sustain me.

¹³Then I will teach transgressors your ways, and sinners will turn back to you. ¹⁴Save me from bloodguilt, O God, the God who saves me, and my tongue will sing of your righteousness. ¹⁵O Lord, open my lips, and my mouth will declare your praise. ¹⁶You do not delight in sacrifice, or I would bring it; you do not take pleasure in burnt offerings. ¹⁷The sacrifices of God are a broken spirit; a broken and contrite heart, O God, you will not despise.

¹⁸In your good pleasure make Zion prosper; build up the walls of Jerusalem. ¹⁹Then there will be righteous sacrifices, whole burnt offerings to delight you; then bulls will be offered on your altar.

1. *Look at the psalm phrase by phrase. What burdens does David carry because of his sin?*

2. *David defiled Bathsheba and murdered Uriah, her husband. Yet what point is he making in verse 4?*

3. *How is this instructive as we consider and confess our own sin? (Psalm 32:1–5)*

4. David's remorse over his sin could have left him wallowing in despair; instead, what hope does he express in verses 13–15? How is this psalm in part an answer to that hopeful prayer?

5. What kinds of sacrifices does God want from us? (vs. 17) How is this illustrated in Luke 18:9–14?

6. What difference does the study of this psalm—the tragedy behind it and God's merciful rescue of David—make in your day-to-day relationship(s)?

7. It has been said that our main job as Christians is not to avoid sin, but to recognize sin. Explain what you think this means.

(Something to think about: are you personally more in danger of underestimating your sins or overestimating them?)

SOMETHING TO THINK ABOUT:

The gospel is proclaimed when we confess and forgive well. Confessing sin is a proclamation that there is a way back from failure, that there is a way to rescue relationships and ourselves from brokenness. We don't have to hide our sin from each other. Forgiveness proclaims that healing is available, that after a sin you don't have to live on a never-ending treadmill hoping to earn your way back into a relationship. In the ordinary moment it forces us to remember and point each other to God's amazing forgiveness.

The reverse is also true. When we refuse to confess and forgive we proclaim hopelessness and despair. We proclaim that the only hope we have of overcoming sin is covering it in the same pointless exercise that Adam and Eve tried at the beginning of the world—and of marriage. We proclaim that sins are never really forgiven but maybe forgotten if enough time goes by and you work and work and work really hard to make the other person feel good about you again. When we ignore God's correction, we lead others astray.

1. What sins are you keeping hidden that you need to confess?

2. *What has kept you from confessing them?*

3. *If you feel that confession should not be made to your spouse, to whom then will you confess the sin?*

One more thing…

Surprise your spouse with a "love note" this week. It can be a store bought card, but be sure to include how you feel about your spouse—what you like, appreciate and admire about him/her. Express thanks for what he/she has done for you.

BUILDING YOUR RELATIONSHIP WITH EACH OTHER

As a couple, complete the following activities and questions.

Read the passage below from Matthew 18:21–35, and then answer the questions.

²¹Then Peter came to Jesus and asked, "Lord, how many times shall I forgive my brother when he sins against me? Up to seven times?"

²²Jesus answered, "I tell you, not seven times, but seventy-seven times. ²³Therefore, the kingdom of heaven is like a king who wanted to settle accounts with his servants. ²⁴As he began the settlement, a man who owed him ten thousand talents was brought to him. ²⁵Since he was not able to pay, the master ordered that he and his wife and his children and all that he had be sold to repay the debt. ²⁶The servant fell on his knees before him. 'Be patient with me,' he begged, 'and I will pay back everything.' ²⁷The servant's master took pity on him, canceled the debt and let him go. ²⁸But when that servant went out, he found one of his fellow servants who owed him a hundred denarii. He grabbed him and began to choke him. 'Pay back what you owe me!' he demanded.

²⁹"His fellow servant fell to his knees and begged him, 'Be patient with me, and I will pay you back.'

³⁰"But he refused. Instead, he went off and had the man thrown into prison until he could pay the debt. ³¹When the other servants saw what had happened, they were greatly distressed and went and told their master everything that had happened.

³²"Then the master called the servant in. 'You wicked servant,' he said, 'I canceled all that debt of yours because you begged me to. ³³Shouldn't you have had mercy on your fellow servant just as I had on you?' ³⁴In anger his master turned him over to the jailers to be tortured, until he should pay back all he owed.

³⁵"This is how my heavenly Father will treat each of you unless you forgive your brother from your heart." (Matthew 18:21–35)

1. *What do you think lies at the heart of Peter's question in verse 21?*

2. *The first servant owes his master a vast sum of money (1 talent = 10 years' wages). Why do you think Jesus uses such an outrageous debt (10,000 talents) for the servant to owe?*

3. *The servant's plea for a chance to pay it all back is absurd. How does the master's action in verse 27 exceed the servant's unrealistic request? How does this action reflect God's treatment of you in Christ? (Colossians 2:13–14)*

4. What was wrong with the servant demanding his 100 denarii back? Why is the master so angry? (Note: 100 denarii = three month's wages)

5. The sum owed by the second servant is nothing in comparison to what the first servant owed. What does the difference in these two debts tell us about God's forgiveness of us, and our forgiveness of others?

6. When you are consumed by your own hurt, where does forgiveness come from?

SOMETHING TO THINK ABOUT:

Our ability to forgive comes from appreciating and living out of God's forgiveness. We have been forgiven a tremendous debt—ten thousand talents' worth, more than you could ever hope to repay. If you don't understand yet how much you've been forgiven, then for now begin to develop an appreciation for it by remembering that your forgiveness required the suffering and death of God's own perfect son. When you appreciate and live out of the joy and gratitude of God's forgiveness, it becomes easier to forgive others. In a sense, you forgive out of the abundance of forgiveness you've received. It isn't about looking inside yourself to find an appropriate emotional response; it's about focusing on God's love and grace and asking for the ability to pass it on to your spouse.

In addressing Christians who were living with all of the challenges of getting along with each other Paul wrote, "Finally, brothers, whatever is true, whatever is noble, whatever is right, whatever is pure, whatever is lovely, whatever is admirable—if anything is excellent or praiseworthy—think about such things" (Philippians 4:8).

1. *Make a list of qualities you like and appreciate about your spouse.*

2. *How has God used him or her to make you more like God? How, then, can you give thanks for your spouse?*

You can build on the ways that you like and appreciate your spouse by considering how he or she has been a blessing to you. This is a bit broader than just considering what you like about your spouse. Being blessed by your spouse includes how God has used him or her to help you grow. How are you a better person because your spouse is in your life?

3. *Are there ways that you find forgiveness especially hard in marriage? Explain.*

4. *Are there ways that you make it more difficult for your spouse to forgive? Be ready to hear what he/she has to share.*

5. *As you consider the aspects of confession and forgiveness addressed in this unit, what have you learned that you can apply in your marriage?*

BEFORE THE NEXT SESSION:

In *Marriage Matters,* read Chapter 15 (pages 217–235).

Unit 8

Building Intimacy

KEY PASSAGE: PSALM 62:5–8

KEY IDEAS:
1. Just as Christ is central to our understanding of marriage, he is central to our understanding of intimacy and sex. The understanding and safety he offers us give us direction in creating intimacy in marriage.
2. Intimacy is established through safety and understanding.
3. When we personally know God's love and acceptance of us, we can love and accept others.
4. Sex is a specific form of intimacy that should grow out of the same foundational elements of intimacy that God offers us.

TO PREPARE FOR THIS SESSION:
In *Marriage Matters,* read Chapter 15 (pages 217–235).

Lesson 8

OPENING

- *List some ways that sex and intimacy are portrayed in the media.*

- *What are some messages about sex and intimacy that we absorb from our culture?*

- *Are the messages different for men than they are for women?*

WHAT IS INTIMACY?

Key Idea: Just as Christ is central to our understanding of marriage, he is central to our understanding of intimacy and sex. The understanding and safety he offers us give us direction in creating intimacy in marriage.

1. *Write your own definition of intimacy.*

2. *List some elements that you think should be present in a relationship for intimacy to exist.*

3. *Read the following Scripture passages and list some aspects of God's intimacy with us.*

> [1]O LORD, you have searched me and you know me. [2]You know when I sit and when I rise; you perceive my thoughts from afar. [3]You discern my going out and my lying down; you are familiar with all my ways. [4]Before a word is on my tongue you know it completely, O LORD. (Psalm 139:1–4)
>
> [9]"I pray for them. I am not praying for the world, but for those you have given me, for they are yours. [10]All I have

is yours, and all you have is mine. And glory has come to me through them. [11]I will remain in the world no longer, but they are still in the world, and I am coming to you. Holy Father, protect them by the power of your name—the name you gave me—so that they may be one as we are one. [12]While I was with them, I protected them and kept them safe by that name you gave me. None has been lost except the one doomed to destruction so that Scripture would be fulfilled.

[13]"I am coming to you now, but I say these things while I am still in the world, so that they may have the full measure of my joy within them. [14]I have given them your word and the world has hated them, for they are not of the world any more than I am of the world. [15]My prayer is not that you take them out of the world but that you protect them from the evil one. [16]They are not of the world, even as I am not of it. [17]Sanctify them by the truth; your word is truth. [18]As you sent me into the world, I have sent them into the world. [19]For them I sanctify myself, that they too may be truly sanctified.

[20]"My prayer is not for them alone. I pray also for those who will believe in me through their message, [21]that all of them may be one, Father, just as you are in me and I am in you. May they also be in us so that the world may believe that you have sent me. [22]I have given them the glory that you gave me, that they may be one as we are one: [23]I in them and you in me. May they be brought to complete unity to let the world know that you sent me and have loved them even as you have loved me." (John 17:9–23)

God, who has called you into fellowship with his Son Jesus Christ our Lord, is faithful. (1 Corinthians 1:9)

CREATING SAFETY AND UNDERSTANDING

Key Idea: Intimacy is established through safety and understanding.

Read Psalm 62:5–8 and discuss the questions that follow.

⁵Find rest, O my soul, in God alone; my hope comes from him. ⁶He alone is my rock and my salvation; he is my fortress, I will not be shaken. ⁷My salvation and my honor depend on God; he is my mighty rock, my refuge. ⁸Trust in him at all times, O people; pour out your hearts to him, for God is our refuge.

1. *Read through these verses and underline every occurrence of the word "my." What does the use of this word indicate about the relationship the psalmist has with God?*

2. *Describe the trust that the psalmist writes about in verse 8. Are there times when it is easier (or harder) for you to trust God?*

Read the following description of intimacy.

Intimacy is about more than sharing things your spouse may not know. It's also about sharing things that you both already do know. Our relationship with God provides a good example of how entrusting another with what he or she already knows is an important part of intimacy. As God becomes intimate with us, he

120 *Unit 8: Building Intimacy*

reveals himself to us and, in turn, asks us to reveal ourselves to him. Obviously, we need him to reveal himself to us; if he didn't choose to reveal himself to us it would be impossible for us to know him. But it seems odd that God would ask us to reveal ourselves to him. After all, he knows absolutely everything about us. In fact, he knows more about us than we know about ourselves!

What's the point of talking to God when he knows what you're going to say before you say it? Nevertheless, God does ask us to pray, and not just to produce a laundry list of wants and needs, but to actively share our deepest thoughts and concerns with him (Psalm 62:8). Many of the psalms consist of the heartfelt cries of joy, anguish, fear, terror, anger, and dismay of God's people. These heartfelt cries weren't shared once and forgotten, but echo through the centuries as God's people, past and present, pour out their hearts to God. God doesn't gain insight or understanding from the psalms or from our personal cries to him, so what's the point? Our relationship with God isn't about telling God something new, it's about entrusting him with what is important to us, and finding that he cares and even delights in it.

Often in marriage, especially as children come into the picture, our communication becomes focused on the logistical needs of the moment. Who is going to pick up the kids from soccer practice? How is Bobby doing in math? How much are Erin's new glasses?

Back when my son Gresham was in kindergarten, each day he would jump off the bus, run inside the house, and inevitably find himself ushered into the kitchen for a debriefing with his mother. As he sipped a cup of juice and downed a few crackers, Kim covered familiar ground. "So what did you do today? What did your teacher say? Did anything funny happen? Did you hear a story? What did you learn?" Neither questions nor answers varied much from day to day. But what amazed me was Kim's response. Her enthusiasm never waned, her questions were always earnest, and every so often tears would even form in her eyes as our son showed her his latest art project. In one sense, Kim wasn't really learning anything from Gresham. She mastered the alphabet, colors, and shapes long ago. And yet she and Gresham were building a relationship, becoming intimate.

Our hearts, and our relationship, can get lost in the details. We become household managers rather than friends and lovers. What you think and feel about the details of your life are critical to really knowing and being intimate with your spouse. But realize, too, that intimacy isn't about just listening for something new, it means being interested in and expressing concern for what you've heard countless times before, remembering that it's been repeated countless times because it's important to your spouse. So before you roll your eyes and remind your spouse that he or she is telling you the same thing you heard yesterday, remind yourself that your spouse is entrusting you with something he or she finds important. Delight in the fact that you are being entrusted again and again with the important matters of your spouse's heart.

For discussion:

- *After reading this description of intimacy, what do you think are some of the key differences between real intimacy (as God portrays it in the Bible) and the way intimacy is portrayed in our culture?*

LOVE AND ACCEPTANCE

Key Idea: When we personally know God's love and acceptance of us, we can love and accept others.

Take some time to think about the characteristics of God's love for us.

> But the fruit of the Spirit is love, joy, peace, patience, kindness, goodness, faithfulness, gentleness and self-control. Against such things there is no law. (Galatians 5:22–23)

> Love is patient, love is kind. It does not envy, it does not boast, it is not proud. It is not rude, it is not self-seeking, it is not easily angered, it keeps no record of wrongs. Love does not delight in evil but rejoices with the truth. It always protects, always trusts, always hopes, always perseveres. (1 Corinthians 13:4–7)

> Accept one another, then, just as Christ accepted you, in order to bring praise to God. (Romans 15:7)

1. *List some characteristics of God's love for you.*

2. *Why do you think acceptance is such an important part of God's love for us and our love for others?*

3. *List some ways Christ accepts you.*

4. *List some of the ways you and your spouse are different from each other.*

5. *How does knowing your own acceptance by Christ impact your acceptance of your spouse's differences?*

Building trust in a relationship requires you to grow in your trust of God. God expresses all of the characteristics you've been reflecting on toward you because of his grace. You can't earn his love, only receive it as a gift in Christ. Take a few moments to pray, affirming your trust in his grace and thanking him for it.

Homework for Unit 8

Key Idea: Sex is a specific form of intimacy that should grow out of the same foundational elements of intimacy that God offers us.

BUILDING YOUR RELATIONSHIP WITH GOD AND WITH EACH OTHER

Work through the homework individually first, then come together with your spouse and go over it together. As you and your spouse work together through the homework remember three important things: first, remember the importance of accepting your spouse and making him/her feel safe. Next, work on speaking the truth in love—share what will most benefit the needs of your spouse and your marriage as a whole. Last, be willing to examine your own heart.

Working through problems of intimacy can be difficult for many reasons. For one, intimacy often seems to be more of an experience than a choice or behavior. It's hard to *do* intimacy. It seems to just happen...or not. How do you control or change something as seemingly wild and unpredictable as intimacy? Intimacy often comes as a surprise. One evening, completely unplanned, you end up sitting on the floor with your spouse looking at old photos, reminiscing, and falling in love all over again. On another evening you hire a babysitter, go out to your favorite restaurant and sit in awkward silence with no idea what to say. Much of what you have been considering and developing in this study are elements of intimacy—honesty, acceptance, getting to know each other better, being willing to share your heart. In this section however, we want to focus in on the physical aspect of intimacy.

Two critical ingredients of intimacy are safety and understanding, but creating both takes effort. Again, thinking carefully about how God offers both as he relates to us can help us take specific steps toward offering them to one another in marriage.

Think back to UNIT 2. Why is worshiping Jesus the answer to building trust and intimacy in your marriage?

HAVE YOU BEEN COMMUNICATING HONESTLY WITH YOUR SPOUSE?

Recall the discussion of Psalm 62:5–8 earlier in the lesson in the section entitled "Creating Safety and Understanding." Reread the passage and ask each other the questions that follow:

1. *Ask: Do you feel safe to communicate and entrust your heart to me?*

2. *Ask: Do I ever seem annoyed with you when you communicate with me?*

3. *Ask: Do I ever seem to judge your heart and intentions?*

SEX AND INTIMACY

Sex can seem mysterious. One spouse wants to have sex more often than the other. One spouse is more adventurous than the other. One spouse enjoys prolonged foreplay and the other doesn't. No one asks for these preferences. Are preferences problems to be solved? Who's to say one spouse's preferences are right and the other's are wrong?

Sex is a subset of intimacy, a particular form of intimacy reserved by God for the most intimate of all human relationships, marriage. And as we shall see, just as Christ is central to our understanding of marriage, so he is central to our understanding of sex.

God intended sex between his image bearers to take place within marriage. The "one-flesh" relationship of marriage described in Genesis 2 is both a picture of an inner connection—a spiritual and psychological intimacy—and a physical connection. Adam and Eve were created to become one at every level. Marriage and sex were designed to go together.

Marriage was created so we could fully image God in the world. To be accurate image bearers, we need to exist in relationships of commitment and love. Jesus is *the* image of God and his relationship with us, his church, is a model we are to follow. Marriage, in particular, mirrors Jesus' relationship with us in unique ways. It is a life-long relationship based on a promise of love and grace that creates oneness.

If marriage is a unique expression of Christ's love for the church and sex is a unique expression of marital love, then shouldn't we, mustn't we, say that marital sex should image Christ's love for the church?

Understanding that God intends sex to be an expression of intimacy has several very important implications.

- **We can't simply think of sex as a function of biology.** We don't have sex simply because we are animals, driven by hard-wired biological urges that we cannot understand. Sex is both a physical experience and an expression of our hearts. In other words, the mysteries of sex are more mysteries of our hearts than mysteries of our bodies. Note: Because sex, obviously, involves biology, it is important to be alert to physical conditions that can contribute to sexual problems. Physical conditions that sometimes contribute to sexual problems include cardiovascular disease, neurological disorders, diabetes, and hormonal imbalances. Also alcohol and drug abuse as well as certain prescribed medications including some antidepressants can have side effects that affect sexual function. You should always consult a physician if you suspect that there are physiological factors affecting sexual intimacy.

- **The quality of our relational intimacy will shape our sexual intimacy**. When we don't connect well "on the inside" we aren't likely to connect well "on the outside." A lack of intimacy in other areas of marriage will often result in problems of sexual intimacy. As many wives have tried to instruct their husbands, "Sex begins in the kitchen." In other words, good sex doesn't just happen in the bedroom; the foundation for good sex is built with loving, caring interactions in every other room of the house. So solving problems of sexual intimacy often means tracing problems of intimacy in the bedroom back to their roots in problems of intimacy in the rest of the relationship. An impatient, angry husband in the family room will often be an impatient, angry lover. A wife who has trouble expressing her wants and desires in the den will often have trouble expressing wants or desires in the bedroom.

- **Understanding how to improve intimacy in the bedroom means learning intimacy from Christ**. The way Christ builds trust and intimacy with us teaches us how to build trust and intimacy with our spouses. And as always, this involves more than simply imitating Jesus. It means worshiping him.

1. *During the group session you were asked to make a list of some elements that must be present in a relationship for intimacy to exist. Compare your list with your spouse's.*

2. *As a couple, discuss how the elements you described for developing intimacy at the beginning of this chapter are also necessary for physical intimacy.*

Think for a moment about the basic mechanics of sex. Husband and wife disrobe, allowing another to see them as few, if any, have ever seen them in their adult lives. There is, quite literally, nowhere to hide, no way to defend yourself from a critical eye or a violent hand. It would be devastating to be laughed at or criticized. You want to be physically valued, accepted, and embraced. What follows is mutual contact. You touch and allow yourself to be touched on the most sensitive parts of your body. The husband enters his wife, literally touching her on the inside. You give the other the power to bless you with pleasure and warmth—or to harm you in a terrible way. Can you see how safety and acceptance are important?

How about service or sacrifice? You may have noticed that men and women respond at different rates, men typically able to climax much more quickly than women. If a man wants to be selfish, he can do so easily, leaving his wife unsatisfied, frustrated, and feeling used. To please his wife, a husband needs self-control, not because it's easy but because he wants to serve and bless his wife by pleasing her.

How about honesty and communication? Husbands and wives have their own preferences, wanting to be touched in some ways and not others. Without good communication, both verbal and nonverbal, how do you know if you are giving your spouse pleasure? How does your spouse know how to love you if you don't communicate it?

Almost every characteristic of heart-level intimacy has a critical counterpart in the area of physical intimacy. The outer is always a fruit of the inner. You might notice, too, that we've already learned how to strengthen many of the elements for intimacy. Learning to honor rather than manipulate your spouse fosters intimacy. Learning how to speak the truth in love fosters intimacy. Learning how to navigate conflict well fosters intimacy.

Explain to one another what is meant by the phrase: "The outer is always a fruit of the inner."

CREATING SAFETY AND UNDERSTANDING IN COMPANIONSHIP

Sometimes we make intimacy almost impossible by trying to conjure it out of thin air. But intimacy must be *about* something; it must have a foundation. Trying to create intimacy out of your desire for intimacy doesn't work any more than trying to create friendship out of an enthusiasm for friendship. Finding simple things to enjoy together and making them a priority may rebuild some of the intimacy you once felt in your relationship. Intimacy isn't a luxury; it's an important part of worshiping God through your marriage—loving him by loving each other as he loves you.

1. *What interests, joys, or enthusiasms do you enjoy with your spouse? (If you can't think of any, go back to when you first met: What brought you together? What did you enjoy doing together?)*

2. *Brainstorm together a list of things that you might enjoy doing together. During the brainstorming process don't be critical, just write down as many as you can as soon as they come to mind. Keep it simple at first: walking the dog, grocery shopping, playing cards, backgammon, or even reading together!*

3. *What act of service can you do together? How could you spend time together with God?*

LET'S CELEBRATE…

Another way to describe marital intimacy is with the word *celebration*. The love that God has given us in Jesus truly is something to be excited about and to celebrate. It is a love so supreme and powerful that when we are really in tune with it, it just has to find physical expression. One of the images that we find in many places in the Bible is the return of Jesus portrayed as a wedding feast. The book of Revelation gives us this wonderful image:

> Then I heard what sounded like a great multitude, like the roar of rushing waters and like loud peals of thunder, shouting: "Hallelujah! For our Lord God Almighty reigns. Let us rejoice and be glad and give him glory! For the wedding of the Lamb has come, and his bride has made herself ready. Fine linen [meaning the righteous acts of the saints], bright and clean, was given her to wear." (Revelation 19:6–8)

Tell each other how you feel about the level of intimacy in your marriage. Be open to hear what your spouse has to say. Discuss things you could do as a couple to increase the level if necessary.

BEFORE THE NEXT SESSION:

In *Marriage Matters*, read Chapter 14 (pages 193–216).

Unit 9

Marriage Roles

KEY PASSAGE: EPHESIANS 5:18–33

KEY IDEAS:
1. An understanding of God's view of authority and servanthood is essential to a discussion of marriage roles from a biblical perspective. If authority is going to serve God's purpose in our relationships, then we must anchor all of our understanding in the foundation of servanthood that Jesus laid.
2. God calls husbands to love their wives as Christ loved the church and gave himself for her.
3. God calls wives to submit to their husbands as they submit to the Lord.
4. However you define them, your marriage roles must reflect the character of Christ.
5. Loving your spouse in their role includes knowing your spouse and valuing their individual gifts and abilities.

TO PREPARE FOR THIS SESSION:
In *Marriage Matters*, read Chapter 14 (pages 193–216).

Lesson 9

OPENING

Spend a few minutes discussing the following questions:

- *What messages about the role of the husband and the role of the wife do we get from our culture?*

- *What is your impression of what the Bible says about marriage roles?*

JESUS' AUTHORITY AND SERVANTHOOD

Key Idea: An understanding of God's view of authority and servanthood is essential to a discussion of marriage roles from a biblical perspective. If authority is going to serve God's purpose in our relationships then we must anchor all of our understanding in the foundation of servanthood that Jesus laid.

Jesus and Authority

Jesus recognized two things about authority: first, it exists for the benefit of those who live under it, and second, it must be an expression of love. As Jesus' followers, our understanding and expression of authority should be as radical, surprising, and utterly other-oriented as Jesus'.

Read Mark 10:35–45 and discuss the questions below.

> ³⁵Then James and John, the sons of Zebedee, came to him. "Teacher," they said, "we want you to do for us whatever we ask."
> ³⁶"What do you want me to do for you?" he asked.
> ³⁷They replied, "Let one of us sit at your right and the other at your left in your glory."
> ³⁸"You don't know what you are asking," Jesus said. "Can you drink the cup I drink or be baptized with the baptism I am baptized with?"
> ³⁹"We can," they answered.
> Jesus said to them, "You will drink the cup I drink and be baptized with the baptism I am baptized with, ⁴⁰but to sit at my right or left is not for me to grant. These places belong to those for whom they have been prepared."
> ⁴¹When the ten heard about this, they became indignant with James and John. ⁴²Jesus called them together and said, "You know that those who are regarded as rulers of the Gentiles lord it over them, and their high officials exercise authority over them. ⁴³Not so with you. Instead, whoever wants to become great among you must be your servant, ⁴⁴and whoever wants to be first must be slave of all. ⁴⁵For even the Son of Man did not come to be served, but to serve, and to give his life as a ransom for many."

1. How do James and John recognize Jesus' authority by their question?

2. What do James and John want from Jesus? Why?

3. Explain Jesus' response, "You don't know what you are asking?" What inaccurate view of authority do James and John have?

4. What do you think it looks or sounds like to "lord it over" (vs. 42) someone?

5. *According to Jesus, how should his followers exercise authority?*

Jesus and Servanthood

Reread Mark 10:45, above, with the following passages:

> ⁴[Jesus] got up from the meal, took off his outer clothing, and wrapped a towel around his waist. ⁵After that, he poured water into a basin and began to wash his disciples' feet, drying them with the towel that was wrapped around him. ⁶He came to Simon Peter, who said to him, "Lord, are you going to wash my feet?" ⁷Jesus replied, "You do not realize now what I am doing, but later you will understand"… ¹²When he had finished washing their feet, he put on his clothes and returned to his place. "Do you understand what I have done for you?" he asked them. ¹³"You call me 'Teacher' and 'Lord,' and rightly so, for that is what I am. ¹⁴Now that I, your Lord and Teacher, have washed your feet, you also should wash one another's feet. ¹⁵I have set you an example that you should do as I have done for you. ¹⁶Very truly I tell you, no servant is greater than his master, nor is a messenger greater than the one who sent him. ¹⁷Now that you know these things, you will be blessed if you do them." (John 13:4–7, 12–17)

> ¹If you have any encouragement from being united with Christ, if any comfort from his love, if any fellowship with the Spirit, if any tenderness and compassion, ²then make my joy complete by being like-minded, having the same love,

being one in spirit and purpose. ³Do nothing out of selfish ambition or vain conceit, but in humility consider others better than yourselves. ⁴Each of you should look not only to your own interests, but also to the interests of the others.

⁵Your attitude should be the same as that of Christ Jesus: ⁶Who, being in very nature God, did not consider equality with God something to be grasped, ⁷but made himself nothing, taking the very nature of a servant, being made in human likeness. ⁸And being found in appearance as a man, he humbled himself and became obedient to death—even death on a cross! ⁹Therefore God exalted him to the highest place and gave him the name that is above every name, ¹⁰that at the name of Jesus every knee should bow, in heaven and on earth and under the earth, ¹¹and every tongue confess that Jesus Christ is Lord, to the glory of God the Father. (Philippians 2:1–11)

1. *What do these passages have in common?*

2. *Based on these passages, what attitudes and characteristics define a servant?*

3. How do these passages help us appreciate God's grace toward us?

THE ROLE OF THE HUSBAND

Key Idea: God calls husbands to love their wives as Christ loved the church and gave himself for her.

Read the passage from Ephesians and discuss the questions that follow.

> [21]Submit to one another out of reverence for Christ.... [25]Husbands, love your wives, just as Christ loved the church and gave himself up for her [26]to make her holy, cleansing her by the washing with water through the word, [27]and to present her to himself as a radiant church, without stain or wrinkle or any other blemish, but holy and blameless. [28]In this same way, husbands ought to love their wives as their own bodies. He who loves his wife loves himself. [29]After all, no one ever hated his own body, but he feeds and cares for it, just as Christ does the church—[30]for we are members of his body. [31]"For this reason a man will leave his father and mother and be united to his wife, and the two will become one flesh." [32]This is a profound mystery—but I am talking about Christ and the church. [33]However, each one of you also must love his wife as he loves himself. (Ephesians 5:21, 25–33a)

1. *How many times does some form of the word* love *appear in this passage?*

2. *To what is a husband's love compared?*

3. *In this most detailed instruction to husbands found in the Bible, why do you think Paul doesn't provide a list of responsibilities, but instead emphasizes the husband's call to love?*

4. *In what ways can you begin to sacrifice for your wife so that she is loved and cared for as Christ loves and cares for us?*

5. *Name some ways that a husband can go wrong in his exercise of authority.*

THE ROLE OF THE WIFE

Key Idea: God calls wives to submit to their husbands as they submit to the Lord.

Having an accurate understanding of biblical authority makes it much easier to understand what submission looks like in a marriage. Read the passage and answer the accompanying questions:

> [18]Be filled with the Spirit.... [22]Wives, submit to your husbands as to the Lord. [23]For the husband is the head of the wife as Christ is the head of the church, his body, of which he is the Savior. [24]Now as the church submits to Christ, so also wives should submit to their husbands in everything.... [33]and

the wife must respect her husband. (Ephesians 5:18b, 22–24, 33b).

1. *What are wives instructed to do? What does this look like? (Consider again, Jesus' own example.)*

2. *In submitting to their husbands, to whom are wives ultimately submitting? (vs. 22)*

3. *Where does the power to submit come from? (vs. 18)*

4. *List some temptations to sin in the area of submitting to authority.*

5. *Does submission mean silence? Read the passage from Psalm 13 and decide whether or not David is submitting to God in how he prays:*

   ¹How long, O Lord? Will you forget me forever? How long will you hide your face from me? ²How long must I wrestle with my thoughts and every day have sorrow in my heart? How long will my enemy triumph over me? ³Look on me and answer, O Lord, my God. Give light to my eyes, or I will sleep in death. (Psalm 13:1–3)

6. *Thinking back to the principles of conflict (UNIT 6), share some ways to correct or question your husband that communicate respect and love.*

When you are struggling in your relationship with your husband, return to that principle. In the context of the role God has given you in your marriage, ask yourself: How am I expressing love to my husband and encouraging him to mature into the image of Christ?

REMEMBER YOUR COMMON CALLING

Key Idea: However you define them, your marriage roles must reflect the character of Christ.

Read the following passage from 1 Peter:

> [21]To this you were called, because Christ suffered for you, leaving you an example, that you should follow in his steps. [22]"He committed no sin, and no deceit was found in his mouth." [23]When they hurled their insults at him, he did not retaliate; when he suffered, he made no threats. Instead, he entrusted himself to him who judges justly. [24]He himself bore our sins in his body on the tree, so that we might die to sins and live for righteousness; by his wounds you have been healed. [25]For you were like sheep going astray, but now you have returned to the Shepherd and Overseer of your souls.
>
> [1]Wives, in the same way be submissive to your husbands so that, if any of them do not believe the word, they may be won over without words by the behavior of their wives, [2]when they see the purity and reverence of your lives....
>
> [7]Husbands, in the same way be considerate as you live with your wives, and treat them with respect as the weaker partner and as heirs with you of the gracious gift of life, so that nothing will hinder your prayers. (1 Peter 2:21—3:2, 7)

Peter begins his instruction to both wives and husbands (3:1, 7) using the phrase: "in the same way." To what does this phrase refer? In the same way as what?

The gist of what Peter writes is that whatever your role, whether leading, following, or both, you are called to look to Jesus, not merely as your example, but most importantly as the only one who can empower you to live out your ultimate calling to love.

In writing to people who were squabbling about their roles in the church, Paul said,

> If I speak in the tongues of…angels, but have not love, I am only a resounding gong or a clanging cymbal.…and if I have a faith that can move mountains, but have not love, I am nothing. (1 Corinthians 13:1–2)

No matter what your role is, no matter how important you think your job is, no matter how good you are at it, if you're not acting in love, then what you do has no value. **No matter how marriage roles are defined, they are only different expressions of love.**

Homework for Unit 9

Key Idea: Loving your spouse in their role includes knowing your spouse and valuing their individual gifts and abilities.

Complete this homework before the next session. (Notice, husband and wife, that you have individual homework tailored just for you.) Record your thoughts and responses below and bring it to the group meeting.

HUSBANDS: BUILDING YOUR RELATIONSHIP WITH GOD

On your own, read the following pages and complete all the activities and questions.

Reread the following Bible passages from the lesson: Mark 10:35–45; John 13:4–7, 12–17; Philippians 2:1–11; and Ephesians 5:18, 21–33.

Keeping Jesus' perspective on servanthood and authority in mind, consider these questions:

1. *Think of some specific instances where it has been difficult for you to love your wife as Christ loves the church.*

2. *Think of specific ways you can display more of a servant's attitude in your marriage.*

Pray and ask for God's grace and wisdom so that you can love and serve your wife in the way God wants you to.

HUSBANDS: SOMETHING TO THINK ABOUT:

In relationships we are always moving toward others, away from others, or against others. Love can move us in any of these directions, but when we find ourselves regularly moving in one direction rather than the others it can be a sign that we aren't following love, but the desires and fears of our hearts that may have become idols.

- Idols can move us toward our wives. When our hearts are ruled by desires or fears, we cave in to every whim or desire

of our wives, all the while thinking we are serving as Christ does.
- Idols can drive us away from our wives. We can exercise our authority in a distancing way, only showing up in our marriage to say no to the things that inconvenience or trouble us, while otherwise being underinvolved.
- Idols can move us against our wives. We can be cruel tyrants, demanding and controlling the details of home life out of our lust for power and control or out of our fear of rejection and failure.

Every area of marriage is an expression of worship, either reflecting your love for God or your love for something else. Often a battle that seems to be about marriage roles is, instead, about deep heart issues.

Questions:

1. *In which direction do you most often tend to move: toward your wife, away from her, or against her? Is there a fear or selfish desire that is motivating the direction?*

2. *Try to think of one thing you can work on so that there is balance in your movement.*

3. *What have you been unwilling to do or let go of because you saw it as "unmanly"?*

4. *What should you be doing in view of the truth that your first duty is to love and to serve?*

A good way to start serving your wife is to ask her to tell you some ways she would like to be helped. This might include something practical like sorting through finances, or something more personal like spending time talking at the end of the day.

WIVES: BUILDING YOUR RELATIONSHIP WITH GOD

On your own, read the following pages and complete all the activities and questions.

Reread the following Bible passages from the lesson: Mark 10:35–45; John 13:4–7, 12–17; Philippians 2:1–11; and Ephesians 5:18, 21–33.

Keeping Jesus' perspective on submission in mind, consider whether or not you respect your husband.

1. Ask your husband if he thinks you respect him.

2. Ask him what it is you do that makes him feel respected.

3. Ask him what you do that makes him feel that you don't respect him.

Understand respect as a form of love.

In relationships where one member has authority, it is important to recognize that respect is an important element of loving the one in authority. In addition to urging wives to submit to their husbands, Paul also reminds them to show respect (Ephesians 5:33).

Act in love even when you are disappointed.

Instead of turning from your husband in disappointment, can you think of a way you can turn toward him with encouragement, a kind word, even your prayers? The shortcomings of your husband can be an opportunity to stroke your own pride or sense of spiritual superiority and indulge in good old-fashioned grumbling. These responses reveal a lack of respect for God more than a lack of respect for your husband. Remember, you have a Savior who trusted God in his worst moments. He can help you in those moments when your trust is running low.

1. *What qualities do you most appreciate and respect in your husband? Do you communicate to him your appreciation and respect for these qualities?*

2. *Do you tend to support and encourage your husband or do you tend to challenge or demean him?*

3. *Have you been able to respect your husband in spite of mistakes?*

Important: Love speaks, exhorts, corrects, and says no to evil. If you or your children are being verbally, physically, or sexually abused, love your husband by saying no to his sin. You need help to do this. Please turn to a trusted family member, friend, pastor, and/or counselor to get the support that you need.

WIVES: SOMETHING TO THINK ABOUT:

Remember that in relationships we are always moving toward others, away from others, or against others. Love can move us in any one of those three directions. But when we find ourselves regularly moving in one direction rather than the others it can be a sign that we aren't following love, but desires and fears of our hearts that may have become idols.

- When our hearts are ruled by desires or fears that move us toward others we can become wives who live to serve our husband's every desire while really serving our own desire for acceptance or living in fear of our husband's wrath, all the while calling it submission.
- Idols can drive us away from others. Wives can use their husband's authority to avoid the difficult conversations, conflicts, and decision making that following Christ requires, by asking the one in authority to fight all of their battles for them and shelter them from life.
- Idols can move us against one another. Wives can pick apart their husband's authority by second-guessing every

move and being critical out of their own distrust or cravings for control.

Every area of marriage is an expression of worship, either reflecting your love for God or your love for something else. Often a battle over marriage roles is really about much deeper heart issues.

Questions:

1. *In which direction do you tend to move: away from your husband, toward him, or against him?*

2. *Try to think of one thing you can work on so that there is balance in your movement.*

3. *What have you been unwilling to do or let go of because you saw it as your "womanly duty"?*

4. *What should you be doing in view of the truth that your first duty is to love and to serve?*

A good way to start serving your husband is to ask him to tell you some ways he would like to be helped. This might include something as practical as sorting through finances or something more personal like spending time talking at the end of the day.

BUILDING YOUR RELATIONSHIP WITH EACH OTHER

Together, read the following pages and complete all the activities and questions.

God gives authority to some to ensure that in every arena of relationship someone is present who is responsible for the care of others. It is a responsibility we all share in at the most basic level, the duty to love, and we may delegate certain duties that need special attention or ability (income versus childcare, etc.), but the one in authority has an added responsibility to make sure needs in *every* area are being met. Even if everyone else is dropping the ball, the one with authority is required to notice and take action.

Paul introduces the issue of authority in relationships in Ephesians 5, by writing,

> Be filled with the Spirit. Speak to one another with
> psalms, hymns and spiritual songs. Sing and make music
> in your heart to the Lord, always giving thanks to God
> the Father for everything, in the name of our Lord Jesus

Christ. Submit to one another out of reverence for Christ. (Ephesians 5:18b–21)

As we live in relationship with each other, guided by the Spirit of Jesus, we should live "musical" lives with each other. Our words and actions should be hymns of praise to God and encouragement to each other. Part of that music is a willingness to submit to one another, even as Christians, in relationships structured by authority. It should look and sound much more like a beautiful dance than a forced march.

In the marriage dance, the husband leads as he listens to the music of Christ. The wife hears the same music and thus they are able to keep time in their own minds and coordinate their steps, all the while enjoying themselves. In a clumsy moment one may step on the toes of the other, and steps have to be reviewed and maybe an instructor consulted, but those moments don't make up what the dance is all about.

There is no simple, one-size-fits-all "to do" list for husbands and wives. Instead of giving you a list of set duties, God, in the Bible, does something much better. He gives a few basic principles to help you and your spouse define your roles in a godly way no matter what your life is like.

1. *List the different responsibilities and roles that you have assumed in your marriage. Describe how each is an expression of God's love.*

2. *If you're having difficulty sorting out your marriage roles, ask a simple question: how has God gifted us?*

3. *Together, create something that describes how your marriage has grown as a result of your time spent on this curriculum. It could be written, or recorded or videoed. Make it in such a way that it can shared with others—family members, young couples or newlyweds, your church leaders.*

BEFORE THE NEXT (THE LAST) SESSION:

In *Marriage Matters*, read Chapters 17 and 18 (pages 253–281).

Unit 10

Keep Your Eyes on the Prize

KEY PASSAGE: HEBREWS 12:1–3

KEY IDEAS:

1. To stay on track in marriage, place your hope in Christ. Find joy and meaning in him, and don't just focus on your spouse.
2. Being called to faith isn't a rebuke for negative emotions or an exhortation to positive thinking, but a call to focus on God's promises, love, and faithfulness even when they aren't visible.
3. Faith means looking to the Savior whose arms never grow tired.
4. Remembering—by faith—is an important part of worshiping God and protecting our hearts and our marriages.
5. Having a positive sense of your marital history isn't just a matter of getting your facts straight, but of letting God provide an interpretive framework of meaning and purpose that provides hope and connects you to Jesus.

TO PREPARE FOR THIS SESSION:

In *Marriage Matters*, read Chapters 17 and 18 (pages 253–281).

Lesson 10

OPENING

As we move into this last lesson consider the following:

- *Write a definition for hope.*

- *What difference does hope make?*

- *Name one thing you hope for in your marriage.*

- *Are there things you have placed too much hope in? What has been the result?*

PRACTICING HOPE

Key Idea: To stay on track in marriage, place your hope in Christ. Find joy and meaning in him, and don't just focus on your spouse.

Never allow yourself to think that your actions make no difference; that they won't change anything. One of the most important actions you can take is to make a daily decision about what you are hoping *for*. Hope is more than a feeling; it is something you do.

Read these passages from Matthew and answer the questions that follow.

> [19]"Do not store up for yourselves treasures on earth, where moth and rust destroy, and where thieves break in and steal. [20]But store up for yourselves treasures in heaven, where moth and rust do not destroy, and where thieves do not break in and steal. [21]For where your treasure is your heart will be also." (Matthew 6:19–21)

> "The kingdom of heaven is like treasure hidden in a field. When a man found it, he hid it again, and then in his joy went and sold all he had and bought that field." (Matthew 13:44)

1. In Matthew 6, what is Jesus cautioning us not to put our hope in?

2. What can happen to our earthly treasures?

3. What is the danger of placing our hope in earthly things?

4. What should we set our hearts on?

5. What do you think of when you think of heavenly treasure?

6. In what ways do you find the kingdom of heaven (God's rule, power, and presence in our lives) a treasure in your life?

7. In what ways is the kingdom of heaven hidden?

8. To what lengths did the man in Matthew 13 go to gain the treasure?

9. *What was the man's attitude when he realized that the treasure lay within his grasp?*

Keeping your eyes on the prize means that in moments when your actions don't seem to matter, you choose to place your hope in Jesus rather than anywhere else. You choose to believe that Jesus is the real treasure—not your spouse or anything else.

YOU'VE GOTTA HAVE FAITH

Key Idea: Being called to faith isn't a rebuke for negative emotions or an exhortation to positive thinking, but a call to focus on God's promises, love, and faithfulness even when they aren't visible.

You need faith in God to stay on the path in a difficult marriage. Faith is more than a feeling that everything is going to turn out all right. Hebrews 11 gives us one of the most detailed studies on faith in the entire Bible.

> [1]Now faith is being sure of what we hope for and certain of what we do not see. [2]This is what the ancients were commended for. [3]By faith we understand that the universe was formed at God's command, so that what is seen was not made out of what was visible.
> [4]By faith Abel offered God a better sacrifice than Cain did. By faith he was commended as a righteous man, when God spoke well of his offerings. And by faith he still speaks, even though he is dead.

⁵By faith Enoch was taken from this life, so that he did not experience death; he could not be found, because God had taken him away. For before he was taken, he was commended as one who pleased God. ⁶And without faith it is impossible to please God, because anyone who comes to him must believe that he exists and that he rewards those who earnestly seek him.

⁷By faith Noah, when warned about things not yet seen, in holy fear built an ark to save his family. By his faith he condemned the world and became heir of the righteousness that comes by faith.

⁸By faith Abraham, when called to go to a place he would later receive as his inheritance, obeyed and went, even though he did not know where he was going. ⁹By faith he made his home in the promised land like a stranger in a foreign country; he lived in tents, as did Isaac and Jacob, who were heirs with him of the same promise. ¹⁰For he was looking forward to the city with foundations, whose architect and builder is God.

¹¹By faith Abraham, even though he was past age—and Sarah herself was barren—was enabled to become a father because he considered him faithful who had made the promise. ¹²And so from this one man, and he as good as dead, came descendants as numerous as the stars in the sky and as countless as the sand on the seashore.

¹³All these people were still living by faith when they died. They did not receive the things promised; they only saw them and welcomed them from a distance. And they admitted that they were aliens and strangers on earth. ¹⁴People who say such things show that they are looking for a country of their own. ¹⁵If they had been thinking of the country they had left, they would have had opportunity to return. ¹⁶Instead, they were longing for a better country—a heavenly one. Therefore God is not ashamed to be called their God, for he has prepared a city for them. (Hebrews 11:1–16)

1. *What is it we hope for as Christians?*

2. *What are things we currently do not see?*

3. *Was the faith the "ancients were commended for" (vs. 2) an emotion or an action? (If you can, read the entire chapter in your Bible.) Explain.*

4. *Seeing faith as a decision, how might it play an important role in your marriage?*

The actions of faith flow out of a focus on God's goodness, power, and activity. You take actions in faith because, through Jesus' sacrifice, God acted to give you a new heart. Why would you respond to your spouse's harshness with gentleness? Why would you choose to speak truth when it would be easier to remain silent? Why would you undertake an act of kindness when kindness won't be returned? Because you believe there is another actor on the scene. Though you can't see him with your eyes, you remember that he is good and rewards those who seek him (Hebrews 11:6).

FAITH AND ACTION

Key Idea: Faith means looking to the Savior whose arms never grow tired.

Read the following passages about Israel's battle with the Amalekites. God has just freed the Israelites from captivity in Egypt. In the plagues, Israel has seen amazing displays of God's power. God has been visibly active and has proven his love. Now God asks the Israelites to do more than just observe his activity and power:

> [17]Remember what the Amalekites did to you along the way when you came out of Egypt. [18]When you were weary and worn out, they met you on your journey and cut off all who were lagging behind; they had no fear of God. (Deuteronomy 25:17–18)

> [8]The Amalekites came and attacked the Israelites at Rephidim. [9]Moses said to Joshua, "Choose some of our men and go out to fight the Amalekites. Tomorrow I will stand on top of the hill with the staff of God in my hands."
> [10]So Joshua fought the Amalekites as Moses had ordered, and Moses, Aaron and Hur went to the top of the hill. [11]As long as Moses held up his hands, the Israelites were winning, but whenever he lowered his hands, the Amalekites were winning. [12]When Moses' hands grew tired, they took a stone and put it under him and he sat on it. Aaron and Hur held his

hands up—one on one side, one on the other—so that his hands remained steady till sunset. ¹³So Joshua overcame the Amalekite army with the sword. (Exodus 17:8–13)

1. *How did Israel feel physically when God called them to go to battle with Amalek? Did Israel feel up to the task?*

2. *Why does Moses stand on the hill with the staff outstretched? (Read Exodus 4:1–5.)*

3. *What determines the outcome of the battle?*

4. *What does it mean that God requires Moses to hold his arms up in order for the battle to be won?*

5. *Describe how Moses, in this story, is a picture of Jesus.*

Hebrews 11 reaches a crescendo in chapter 12 as we are reminded of what a great Savior we have in Jesus.

> Let us fix our eyes on Jesus, the author and perfecter of our faith, who for the joy set before him endured the cross, scorning its shame, and sat down at the right hand of the throne of God. (Hebrews 12:2)

In Jesus we have a Savior who has known and lived through all of our battles without faltering or failing. Jesus stretched out his arms—in a very different way—on our behalf.

FOCUSING ON THE REAL STORY— GOD'S WORK

Key Idea: Remembering—by faith—is an important part of worshiping God and protecting our hearts and our marriages.

As Israel prepares to enter the Promised Land, God calls them together and tells their story from his perspective.

> ²Remember how the LORD your God led you all the way in the desert these forty years, to humble you and to test you in order to know what was in your heart, whether or not you would keep his commands. ³He humbled you, causing you to hunger and then feeding you with manna, which neither you nor your fathers had known, to teach you that man does not live on bread alone but on every word that comes from the mouth of the LORD. ⁴Your clothes did not wear out and your feet did not swell during these forty years. ⁵Know then in your heart that as a man disciplines his son, so the LORD your God disciplines you. (Deuteronomy 8:2–5)

1. *What was God's purpose in bringing hardships on his people?*

2. *What is God's purpose for us in our own sufferings?*

3. *In verse 3 what does God say he was teaching the Israelites?*

4. *How can we apply the lesson of the manna to our own lives? Can you think of ways that God has met your needs in ways that you couldn't? In particular, how has he taught you to seek and trust him above all else?*

5. *In the midst of marriage struggles, where do you see signs of God's faithfulness and care? Are there things that appear ordinary, but that, in fact, are God's daily provision of love and grace for you?*

SOMETHING TO THINK ABOUT:

Bread is basic, not very exciting. God wants us to humbly accept what we need and not feed our lusts by providing us with everything we want. There is daily bread all around you. It is easy to overlook, easy to become tired of, but it is what you need. Consider Jesus' words in John 6:

> [32]Jesus said to them, "I tell you the truth, it is not Moses who has given you the bread from heaven, but it is my Father who gives you the true bread from heaven. [33]For the bread of God is he who comes down from heaven and gives life to the world."
> [34]"Sir," they said, "from now on give us this bread."
> [35]Then Jesus declared, "I am the bread of life. He who comes to me will never go hungry, and he who believes in me will never be thirsty." (John 6:32–35)

Like every aspect of our lives, our memories are shaped by the condition of our worshiping hearts. An important part of worshiping God and protecting our hearts and our marriages is remembering by faith. This week, as you revisit your history, look for the ways it reveals your need for Jesus and all of the ways that God has been bringing you to him.

Homework for Unit 10

Key Idea: Having a positive sense of your marital history isn't just a matter of getting your facts straight, but of letting God provide an interpretive framework of meaning and purpose that provides hope and connects you to Jesus.

BUILDING YOUR RELATIONSHIP WITH GOD

On your own, complete these activities and questions.

How can you navigate life's obstacles while keeping your eyes on the prize? In your Bible, reread Hebrews 11. Continue by reading the beginning of Hebrews 12:

> ¹Therefore, since we are surrounded by such a great cloud of witnesses, let us throw off everything that hinders and the sin that so easily entangles, and let us run with perseverance the race marked out for us. ²Let us fix our eyes on Jesus, the author and perfecter of our faith, who for the joy set before him endured the cross, scorning its shame, and sat down at the right hand of the throne of God. ³Consider him who endured such opposition from sinful men, so that you will not grow weary and lose heart. (Hebrews 12:1–3)

1. *Who comprise the "cloud of witnesses" that surrounds us? What do they witness to? What difference does it make for us to consider their lives?*

2. *What image does the author use to picture the Christian life?*

3. *On whom should we fix our gaze as we run our race? What is the danger in being distracted and looking elsewhere?*

4. *What kind of thoughts kept Jesus going in his own race and experience of suffering? (See also Isaiah 50:4–9a.) In the midst of being humiliated and mistreated, what does Jesus focus his thoughts on?*

5. *What common fears do we see in Isaiah 50:4–9a that Jesus overcomes?*

SOMETHING TO THINK ABOUT:

Will you obey and follow Jesus? You are faced with a decision: you can try to find your own way through the dark moments of being sinned against, follow the wisdom of the world, or create your own "light" if you choose. You can try to hide from the pain of being sinned against, launch your own first strike, or find some other compromise. The choice is yours. But Jesus makes it very clear: when you reject his path, his pattern of love, and choose your own, you are in effect rejecting him.

In preparation for "Building Your Relationship with Each Other," think about some of the difficulties you have experienced in your life. What made these situations difficult? Can you identify any patterns?

What may the themes and patterns of these difficulties reveal to you about your own heart? What has God been trying to reveal to you?

BUILDING YOUR RELATIONSHIP WITH EACH OTHER

As a couple, complete the following activities and questions.

Knowing where you've been has everything to do with where you're going.

1. *What is one of your favorite stories as a couple?*

2. *Recall an event in your marriage that really captures the story of your marriage, the highs and the lows, the beauty and the struggles.*

3. *Take some time to remember moments in your marriage where you saw God's faithfulness and care.*

4. *Have there been moments where something wonderful happened unexpectedly?*

5. *Can you think of a time when things turned out better than you thought they would?*

6. *What tangible evidence do you have of God's love and care?*

SOMETHING TO THINK ABOUT:

John Gottman, PhD, a well known researcher and author on the subject of marriage, argues that one measure of the strength of a marriage is how husbands and wives view their past—how they tell their story. Couples that have a positive view of their story are able to maintain a positive view of each other and their marriage. In fact, reflecting on the positives of their history becomes a resource for handling challenges in the present.**

When you reflect on the story of your marriage you actively interpret it, highlighting some parts, downplaying others, choosing words and images that provide a framework of meaning, purpose, and direction. Unhappy couples often remember their story in a

---

**John M. Gottman and Nan Silver, *The Seven Principles for Making Marriage Work* (New York: Three Rivers Press, 1999), 63, 70.

way that highlights the pain and the struggle, and edit out the positive parts, even God himself. Having a positive sense of your marital history isn't just a matter of getting your facts straight, but of letting God provide an interpretive framework of meaning and purpose that provides hope and connects you to Jesus.

IN CLOSING...

1. What have you learned in this marriage course? How have you grown and changed? What has God been doing in you and in your marriage?

2. What are some ways that you understand love better or love your spouse more because you've been through tough times and persevered?

3. *How has God taught you to seek and trust him above all else?*

Leaders Guide

Inviting couples to think and speak publicly and honestly about marriage places you in a position of special responsibility and trust. The couples that you lead through this material will not only be asked to explore what the Bible says about marriage, but to explore their own hearts before the Lord and how that is reflected in the way they treat their spouse. While this is a great opportunity for them, it also makes them vulnerable. They will be vulnerable to the temptations of discouragement, shame, anger, judgment, blame shifting, and more. To ensure that working through this manual is a constructive exercise for their marriage, I suggest the following:

- Before couples commit to being part of a *Marriage Matters* group, make sure that they understand that they will be asked to examine their own hearts and marriages with each other, and at times, with the group. If their marriage is especially volatile and there are regular conflicts that involve verbal attacks and tirades, and especially if there is bullying, physical intimidation, or violence, then using this manual in a small group setting is not the appropriate starting point for them. They should seek help from their pastor or other counselor with appropriate training and experience in marital counseling.
- Emphasize and reinforce the messages outlined in the Introduction about being committed to focusing on their own need to learn and grow and being careful about how they speak about their marriage and especially about their spouse in the context of a group. Undoubtedly, there will be uncomfortable moments, but be proactive as the leader to create a constructive atmosphere. Be alert to how spouses are

responding to each other and to other couples in the group. Don't let discussions get overheated; redirect when you feel it is needed, and follow up with distressed couples afterward.
- You might consider making yourself or some other person or mentoring couple available as a resource between sessions if couples find themselves struggling and needing additional input. That doesn't mean that you need to put yourself in the role of marital counselor, but knowing that it is possible to contact someone for clarification or additional direction between meetings can provide an extra measure of safety and structure if needed.

Pastors or counselors who are using this material to work individually with spouses or couples should feel free to do so creatively, based on what they consider to be immediate or pressing needs. Those using the manual in a group context should consider the following suggested format for going through the units and homework:

1. The manual is designed to be used in coordination with the book, *Marriage Matters: Extraordinary Change through Ordinary Moments.* Emphasize the importance of reading through the corresponding passages in the book before working through the material in the manual. Reading the book will provide the necessary background material for each unit, and the material in the manual will be reinforced and further explained as you progress through the book.
2. Ask couples to read through each unit separately or together before meeting as a group. They may wait to answer questions in the small group, although some couples find it helpful to work through the questions before meeting in a group. At home preparation should be done in whatever way they think would be most helpful and appropriate for them.
3. Ask couples to complete homework from the previous unit before reading through the next unit. Couples will probably need to spend about an hour going through this material during the week.

4. Continue this pattern throughout the course. The first week you will go through Unit 1 and couples will be asked to complete Unit 1 homework. The second week you can discuss the Unit 1 homework (or ask someone to share one thing they learned as they did the homework) before going through Unit 2. The homework is not simply reinforcing the concepts in the lesson, but it also introduces new material. Emphasize the importance of completing the homework from the unit covered in the small group before reading through the next unit.

Suggested Time Frame:

Each lesson is formatted to take 60 minutes in the small group. Homework (both individually and together) will probably take an additional 45–60 minutes.

Leader's Helps:

Notes for each lesson begin below.

Unit 1: Introduction to Marital Change
Lesson 1

OPENING ACTIVITY (10 minutes)

- *List some ordinary irritations and problems of marriage.*

    Leader: You may want to write down the answers so they can be seen by everyone (large paper, white board, etc.).

- *Discuss what makes these things seem so ordinary.*

    Leader notes: Ordinary moments happen over and over. In every difficult situation there is a familiar pattern to how you feel, what you've come to expect, or how you respond. Because these moments happen over and over, it may be hard to detect God's involvement. Perhaps you've never even thought to ask God for help precisely because these moments seem so ordinary. Why bother God with it?

Maybe you're afraid to ask God to get involved because you're ashamed. You feel that you should be able to do better; you feel that God must be disappointed with you.

Or maybe you asked God for help and, it seemed, he remained silent. God's apparent silence after prayer is especially hard. He seems more than uninvolved; he seems to have abandoned or forgotten you.

But whether you've looked for God's help or not, these moments feel ordinary in that there are no miracles and no dramatic changes to be seen. No matter how spiritually minded we may think we are, it is easy to find ourselves doing life on our own, as if God were far, far away.

If you've lived through enough of these ordinary moments without sensing any change, you either become accustomed to the aggravation and indifferent to it, or worse, you slowly sink into hopelessness, no longer harboring any real hope for change. Indifference and hopelessness are both dangerous. The danger isn't simply that you're unhappy or that your marriage is less than it could be; the biggest danger is that God becomes increasingly irrelevant to your marriage, the relationship that defines your life more than any other.

GOD AND LOVE (15 minutes)

1. *What does this passage teach about God?*
2. *How does God show his love to us?*
3. *What does this passage teach about love?*
4. *Why are we to show love to one another?*
5. *What are some ways to apply these truths to marriage?*

Leader notes: This passage identifies three ingredients necessary for the ordinary moments of marriage to become extraordinary moments of change.

1. God is love.

We all want more love in our marriages. For the most part, we marry because of love or at least because we hope for love, but in the most difficult moments we don't feel loved, and we find it hard to love. God may not seem to make much difference in these moments, but his involvement is crucial. God is love, and when you find it hard to love, you need him all the more. A lack of love means that you should not just look more closely at your marriage, but at yourself and at God. If you have any hope of having more love in your marriage, it's going to mean having more of God in your marriage. If you are having trouble loving, either you don't know God or something is interfering with your relationship with God. If we believe that God is love, then he must be the solution for a lack of love.

2. We need to love as God loves.

The Bible tells us that we can actually know some very definite things about love:

a. Love is a person—God. Love can be exciting and feel wonderful, but ultimately, love is a person, not an experience. When you need help loving your spouse, you don't have to wait for the feeling to hit you, long for lost romance, or guess what love is. You can look to God and learn from him. Jesus doesn't just motivate us to love; he teaches how to love in the moment—what it looks like and how to do it.

b. Love is an action. God showed his love by sending his Son.

c. Love is willing to sacrifice. God sacrificed his Son for us.

d. Our love is motivated by God's love toward us: "since God so loved us, we also ought to love one another."

Marriages change when we are willing to love in practical, Christlike ways, especially in the difficult moments. God loves us. God has shown us how to love by his example. The Bible tells us that Jesus is "an atoning sacrifice for our sins." That means that Jesus is able to remove from our hearts all of the obstacles that keep us from love. As much as we say we want to love, sin squashes our best efforts. Jesus isn't just an encouraging coach or an example to follow, but our champion who is able to defeat giants we would never be able to tackle on our own.

3. Grasping the depth of God's love for us, we can then love others. Marriages change when we are willing to love consistently over time, not because our spouses change, but because we are in a growing relationship with God.

LOVE AND GRACE (20 minutes)

GRACE AND MARRIAGE (15 minutes)

Homework for Unit 1

Unit 2: Worship Changes Marriages
Lesson 2

OPENING (10 minutes)

- *Last week we learned that our relationship with our spouse is a window into what? Explain your answer.*

    Your relationship with God, because how you love your spouse reflects how obedient and committed you are to Christ's command to love your neighbor as yourself.

- *What can redeem and transform an ordinary marriage?*

    Committing to love your spouse as Jesus commanded us, because then we are a part of God's agenda and we make God visible.

WHAT DO YOU WORSHIP? (15 minutes)

Leader: You can move through this exercise fairly quickly. It is meant to remind participants of who God is and why he alone is worthy of our worship.

Leader **tip:** You may want to list circled and underlined words and phrases for everyone to see.

1. *Circle the words that describe God's role in the psalmist's life.*

    Refuge, rock, fortress, hope, confidence, relies on God, praises God, comforter

2. *Underline words that describe qualities of God (don't be afraid to underline words that are already circled).*

    Refuge, righteous, ever-present, deliverer, sovereign, strong, splendorous, immeasurable, mighty, marvelous, powerful, unique, faithful, holy

WORSHIP ALWAYS CHANGES YOU (20 minutes)

Leader: List the answers for all to see.

1. *What are some characteristics of idols?*

   They are man-made, worthless, dead, mere objects; they mimic reality but are fakes.

2. *What is the danger of worshiping idols?*

   Those who make them will be like them—dead, fake, worthless.

3. *What is the effect of true worship?*

   True worship has a life-giving effect; it changes us for the better. If we worship God, he will bless us.

   Leader: You can choose to do the questions without rereading if you think everyone in the group is familiar with the vignette.

   Leader: After group discussion, have someone read the following continuation of the account aloud.

WORSHIP IS MORE THAN KNOWING (15 minutes)

Homework for Unit 2

Unit 3: You and Me and Marriage
Lesson 3

OPENING REVIEW (5 minutes)

Leader tip: Be prepared to begin this discussion by sharing what you yourself discovered. If people seem hesitant to open up, you might ask who identified the same idol that you did. Then ask for other attributes of God or Scripture passages they came up with.

THE CREATION AND PURPOSE OF MARRIAGE
(30 minutes)

1. *What does it mean to "image" God? In what ways does God want us to image him?*

   Imaging God means to be like him, to be his representative in creation. We image him by creating offspring, creating order out of disorder, and ruling over what was made.

2. *If God exists as three Persons, and we were created in his image, what is the problem with being alone?*

   We do not mirror his image completely if we are alone because God in his very nature exists in relationship; interaction with equal beings is a part of God's image. Of course, you can mirror his image in all kinds of relationships—not just a marriage relationship.

3. *How should that inform our understanding of God's purpose of marriage?*

   It is intended to mirror the image of God—a married couple is two distinct people who become one in relationship.

4. *Many of the attributes and characteristics of God are on display in relationships. List some of God's characteristics that we should image as we interact with others.*

   Love, kindness, gentleness, patience, forgiveness, compassion, generosity, goodness

SOMETHING TO THINK ABOUT

1. *What is Peter's main idea in verses 20–25?*

   We need to be willing to suffer for doing good, just as Christ did.

2. *What was the purpose of Christ's suffering?*

   Set an example; to return us to God; so that we might die to sins and live for righteousness; to save us

3. *How did Jesus respond to suffering?*

    Did not retaliate; made no threats; entrusted himself to God

4. *What does it mean when Peter says husbands and wives should act "in the same way" in their marriages?*

    Willing to suffer for doing good; not retaliate; not making threats; trusting in God; submissive and considerate

WHOSE PURPOSE DOES YOUR MARRIAGE SERVE? (15 minutes)

Leader notes: *Scenario A is an example of manipulation by punishing.* Sometimes manipulation is easy to spot. The most obvious forms involve "punishing" our spouses for failing to do what we want. There are many ways to punish: silence, criticism, anger, and gossip among others.

Scenario B is an example of manipulation by rewarding. In many ways, Charles was not an angry or difficult husband. In fact, he could be warm and charming, planning surprise getaway weekends, bestowing lavish gifts, and telling Jessica how wonderful she was. For many years Jessica loved this about Charles, but over time his attentions made her feel manipulated. Often, they followed angry arguments or preceded upsetting news. She began to realize that she was being paid off. Charles needed to see beyond the acts, which seemed loving, to his self-serving heart.

"CONSIDER OTHERS BETTER THAN YOURSELVES" (10 minutes)

Homework for Unit 3

Unit 4: Communication: Honesty and Oneness

Lesson 4

OPENING (5 minutes)

Leader: Notice, Paul is saying much more than "stop lying." He is telling us that we must speak the truth. In other words, loving each other doesn't just mean not telling lies; to do that, all you would have to do is remain silent. Paul instructs us to provide each other with honest, accurate information—the truth.

THE PROBLEM OF HIDING (10 minutes)

1. *What is the big change that occurs from Genesis 2:25 to Genesis 3:13?*

   Adam and Eve went from being open, uncovered, unashamed to feeling shame and the need to hide. The nakedness that the Bible is talking about is more than physical nakedness. Adam and Eve's physical nakedness is simply a visible expression of the total openness they enjoyed with each other and God himself. They literally lived with nothing to hide, inside or out.

2. *What did Satan do to cause this fall?*

   He lied.

3. *What did Adam and Eve do that shows they began hiding from each other?*

   They sewed fig leaves together to hide from each other.

4. *What did they do that shows they began hiding from God?*

   They hid among the trees.

5. *What did they do that shows they began hiding from themselves?*

   In a sense they are trying to hide from their own guilt; they also hide from themselves by not admitting directly to their own disobedience—they first blame another.

SPEAKING TRUTH IN LOVE (15 minutes)

3. *What is the result of speaking the truth in love?*

   We will grow up into Christ.

4. *Why do we speak the truth?*

   Because we were created to be like God

5. *What are some evidences of a hardened heart?*

   Ignorance, futility, separation from the life of God; dissatisfaction (continual lust for more)

SPEAKING WITH GRACE AND MERCY (10 minutes)

1. *What allows us to go to Christ with our weaknesses and needs with confidence instead of with fear?*

   He sympathizes with us; he gives us grace and mercy.

2. *How should you imitate Christ's example with your spouse?*

   You also need to sympathize and show grace and mercy.

EMOTIONS: ANGER AND FEAR (20 minutes)

Leader note: Pick and choose which of these questions you will discuss in the small group. Question #4 might be a bit too personal for everyone to share about, but it will still be helpful for participants to answer.

Homework for Unit 4

Unit 5: Constructive Communication

Lesson 5

OPENING (5 minutes)

COMMON FORMS OF DISHONESTY (20 minutes)

COMMON WAYS TO DISTORT THE TRUTH (35 minutes)

1. *According to this verse, what should never come out of our mouths?*

   Unwholesome talk

2. *How can we know if something we say is unwholesome?*

   If it doesn't build others up, isn't according to their needs, and doesn't benefit others

3. *How does this affect how we "tell the truth"?*

   We don't say everything that we think or feel. We choose our words carefully—according to the needs of others, not our own needs.

SOMETHING TO THINK ABOUT:
4. Shaming.

1. *What do all of these ways we distort truth have in common?*

   These are all ways of sinfully protecting ourselves. We take the focus off of ourselves by attacking the identity of our spouses, reducing them to the behavior that has hurt or offended us.

2. *Why don't these distortions of truth ever work?*

   These distortions of truth are manipulative. By using our spouses to defend ourselves we are treating them like objects that exist for us rather than honoring them in love. Ultimately, manipulation only makes things worse.

Homework for Unit 5

Unit 6: Conflict: God Is Up to Something Good

Lesson 6

OPENING (5 minutes)

THE NATURE OF CONFLICT (15 minutes)

1. *What is the source of our quarrels and conflicts?*

   Our own desires—we don't get what we want.

2. *Against who or what do we struggle?*

   Against the spiritual forces of evil; our spouse is not our enemy, Satan and sin are.

3. *According to Ephesians 6 what should be our protection?*

   Truth, righteousness, the gospel of peace, faith, salvation, the sword of the Spirit

4. *If quarrels, as James says, come from the desires within us, where should we begin to bring a positive outcome out of conflict?*

   We should begin by examining ourselves; once we know ourselves as broken image bearers, worshipers gone wrong, rebels against God, we must include ourselves in all of the things that have made our life difficult.

5. *What keeps us from first examining our own hearts?*

   Pride, fear, desire to be right, self-righteousness

6. *What could help you in the midst of conflict to be ready and willing to first "take the plank out of your own eye"?*

   Accepting the fact that we are sinners; accepting that it is good to have our hearts and weaknesses exposed so that we can grow and change; knowing that God gives grace to the humble

HOW DO WE EXAMINE OUR OWN HEARTS?
(15 minutes)

1. *Back to Jack and Michelle: what do you think are the real issues that drive their conflict?*

    It is likely that Michelle wanted more than just "help with the kids." She feels angry because she wants something deeper that hasn't been put on the table for discussion. Perhaps she wants to be treated differently by her husband. Maybe beneath the bedtime event is a sense that her husband doesn't value time with the kids. Or maybe she feels her husband doesn't value or respect her role as a parent. She wants him to express appreciation and respect for what she does, even if he doesn't view those duties as part of his role. Or perhaps, at root, she simply doesn't feel like her husband values her as a wife. It feels that he just views her as domestic help—a nanny, cook, and maid. It isn't so much that she wants him to put the kids to bed with her; she wants her husband to treat her like she is more than hired help. She wants him to want her for her.

2. *How could Michelle have rephrased her complaints to Jack?*

    She could have said something like, "I just realized that when I was angry at you for not helping me put the kids to bed, it was really about something else we need to talk about. But first I want to tell you I'm sorry I snapped at you in my anger. It was wrong, and I ask you to forgive me." Identifying the "want issues" becomes an exercise in removing the plank from your own eye.

3. *What could be some wrong motives for being willing to examine your own heart first?*

    When you are removing a plank from your eye, don't confess something just to make yourself look good or throw your spouse off balance, or so that you can get to pointing out their shortcomings more quickly. If you do, you'll simply be replacing one plank with another. Take the time you need to honestly reflect upon what's going on in your own heart. Think, pray, journal. Sin against a spouse is sin against God. Repent of your sin and trust God to enable you to be Christ-like with your spouse.

4. *When we think of conflict, we sometimes think in terms of a winner and a loser, a stronger and a weaker. How is godly conflict different?*

   Godly conflict exists to create winners and to abolish sin; the purpose is not to destroy the weaker but make him/her stronger and more godly; we face godly conflict as a team not as opponents.

A BIBLICAL APPROACH TO CONFLICT (15 minutes)

THE KEY: LOVE IS MORE THAN RIGHT AND WRONG (10 minutes)

Leader notes: The Corinthian church was beset with problems: disputes over which leaders to follow (1 Cor. 1:10–17); sexual immorality (1 Cor. 5:1); divorce (1 Cor. 7); even how to maintain order during worship services. Paul's letter is full of practical advice. But, wisely, Paul does more than just give instructions on what to do. He gives his readers a principle to guide them in not only solving their current problems, but the many problems that, undoubtedly, would arise in the future.

Paul applies this principle to a very real problem of the early church: there was debate as to whether it was acceptable for Christians to eat foods that had been sacrificed to idols. In the ancient world, pagan religions would sometimes sell meat in the marketplace that had been used in ritual sacrifice. Some Christians had no qualms eating such meat. Others felt that this was wrong, that the meat had been defiled because it had been used in pagan sacrifice. Who was right? How should this conflict be resolved? The issue of ritually sacrificed meat may seem strange, foreign, and irrelevant to us, but Paul's strategies for handling the conflict are very helpful and relevant for dealing with conflict in marriage.

1. *What do you think the apostle Paul was trying to teach the Corinthians when he wrote "knowledge puffs up, but love builds up" (vs. 1)?*

    We can be right in principle, but so wrong in the way we act on that principle that we're harming others and not acting in love. Love always helps others to grow by building them up.

2. *According to Paul, what is the correct answer to whether Christians could eat meat that had been sacrificed to idols?*

    Christians are free to eat the meat sacrificed to idols.

3. *What is the condition Paul places on this "right" to eat the meat? What do the Corinthians need to "be careful" of?*

    That they don't use their freedom to harm others

4. *Which approach to handling conflict should you use?*

    Different approaches according to what would build up your spouse

Homework for Unit 6

Unit 7: Forgiveness
Lesson 7

OPENING (10 minutes)

FORGIVENESS DEFINED (20 minutes)

1. *What does this command reveal about what is important to God?*

    The condition of our relationships with others is important to God. We worship and honor him by loving others.

2. *Why do you think this is important to God? (Think back to UNIT 1.)*

    Our relationships with people are a window into our relationship with God; God loves people, God has paid a price to defeat and overcome sin and so he wants us to treat it seriously and conquer it when we see it as well.

3. *What does this highlight about our worship of God and the act of forgiveness?*

    God is worshiped when we accurately reflect who he is; we cannot accurately reflect the character of God when we are not reconciled with one another.

4. *What images of God's forgiveness can you find in this passage?*

    The temple curtain that separated the people from God was torn in two, blood was shed, hearts are sprinkled clean, and our bodies washed with pure water.

5. *How were these images reminders to the people of God's holiness and their sinfulness?*

    The people's sin separated them from God—displayed by the curtain; God's holiness was displayed by the requirements to be cleansed and to appear before him with the proper clothing; the blood represented the death they deserved for their sin.

6. *How were these images also reminders to the people of God's love for them?*

    They were requirements given by God to allow them to approach him and to be forgiven; the temple was God's dwelling on earth with his people; they were also reminders that God desired a relationship with them.

7. *What then was signified when the curtain was torn in two at Jesus' death?*

    His people had been forgiven once and for all; the obstacle separating them from God was removed.

8. *What do you think is the significance of the dead rising from their graves?*

   Like the curtain being torn, it showed that even death no longer has to separate us from God; like Jesus had victory over our sin, he also had victory over death—the consequence of sin.

9. *What has Jesus' death accomplished?*

   Jesus has become a perfect sacrifice that removes our sins once and for all so that there is no need for a curtain of separation and death. We can now draw near to God in an intimate way, without fear of rejection or judgment.

Leader notes: To understand the significance of the torn temple curtain, remember that sin creates separation at every level of relationship. It separates parent from child, church member from church member, friend from friend, and husband from wife. Sin even divides our own hearts. But nowhere is this separation starker than between God and his people. Apart from Jesus, it is inconceivable that a sinner would approach God without being destroyed. In the law, God encoded and symbolized both this separation and his determination to rescue us. His law contains numerous commands explaining what behaviors made people unclean—unacceptable to God—along with the rituals, washings, and sacrifices required to cleanse. In many instances cleansing required an animal sacrifice; the shedding of its blood signified the seriousness of sin, reminding us that the appropriate punishment for sin is death.

   Once a year, the high priest would make atonement for all of Israel. After careful cleansing, attired in special garments, the high priest entered the Most Holy Place, the inner room, which housed the ark of the Testimony, God's earthly throne (Exodus 25:10–22). This inner room was separated from the rest of the temple by a heavy curtain. In this room the high priest sprinkled the blood of sacrificed animals on the atonement cover of the ark (Leviticus 16:1–19). This annual atonement was done according to God's specific detailed instructions; to do it carelessly would result in immediate death (Leviticus 16:2).

LEARNING TO FORGIVE AS GOD FORGIVES (10 minutes)

HOW FORGIVENESS WORKS (20 minutes)

1. *How might Jonathan feel tempted to punish his wife?*

   He may want to be angry with her; he may be tempted to defend himself in front of Robert and share gossip about his wife; he may be tempted to give his wife "the cold shoulder"; he may be tempted to hold on to it and use it against her later.

2. *What will it look like to release her from any penalty?*

   He will need to confront her about it, be honest about what he is feeling, allow her the opportunity to ask forgiveness, and then choose to release her from any penalty and restore the relationship.

3. *What might he need to sacrifice to be able to release her?*

   He will need to sacrifice the desire to make her pay or use the sin against her; he will need to sacrifice the comfort of just ignoring it; he will need to accept the pain and hurt that was caused.

4. *How can he set his mind to trust God and allow for growth?*

   He will need to trust that God can bring good out of the situation for him, his wife, and Robert; he needs to remember that he too is a sinner in need of mercy and that God is working and is patient; he needs to remember verses like Colossians 3:13.

Homework for Unit 7

Unit 8: Building Intimacy
Lesson 8

OPENING (5 minutes)

Leader: The small group time for this unit will focus on the contrast between the way our culture portrays sex and intimacy and how

God, in his Word, describes intimacy. This will give your small group a way of discussing intimacy in marriage without inappropriate sharing of specific details from their own marriage.

WHAT IS INTIMACY? (20 minutes)

CREATING SAFETY AND UNDERSTANDING (20 minutes)

Leader: You can have your group read Psalm 62:5–8 silently to themselves or have one person read it out loud.

1. *Read through these verses and underline every occurrence of the word "my." What does the use of this word indicate about the relationship the psalmist has with God?*

   "My" indicates intimacy between the psalmist and God.

   Leader: You can have your group read the description of intimacy silently to themselves or have one person read it out loud.

LOVE AND ACCEPTANCE (15 minutes)

Homework for Unit 8

Unit 9: Marriage Roles
Lesson 9

OPENING (10 minutes)

Leader: You may want to divide up into same sex groups for this lesson. It can be helpful to have an older woman leading the women and an older man leading the men in your discussion of marriage roles.

JESUS' AUTHORITY AND SERVANTHOOD
Jesus and Authority (10 minutes)

1. *How do James and John recognize Jesus' authority by their question?*

   They realize Jesus has the authority to offer these positions; they recognize that Jesus will rule one day on a throne.

2. *What do James and John want from Jesus? Why?*

   They want to have authority, recognition, power; perhaps they are even picturing ease and comfort.

3. *Explain Jesus' response, "You don't know what you are asking?" What inaccurate view of authority do James and John have?*

   Jesus neither denies that he has the authority, nor does he deny the existence of authority, but he does say that being in authority is not about ease and comfort, power and glory. Authority requires sacrifice, responsibility, and testing.

4. *What do you think it looks or sounds like to "lord it over" (vs. 42) someone?*

   Some ideas may include: demanding submission or the other person's service; showing disrespect to the person you have authority over; expecting or demanding that things be done your way.

5. *According to Jesus, how should his followers exercise authority?*

   By serving others; when Jesus exercises his authority he assumes the position of a servant, meeting people at their level, assuming their station in life, doing without for their benefit, making decisions for their welfare.

Jesus and Servanthood (10 minutes)

1. *What do these passages have in common?*

   Both are talking about how Jesus used his authority to serve.

2. *Based on these passages, what attitudes and characteristics define a servant?*

   Being willing to give up your own life, being willing to do the hard work of serving someone practically (washing their feet), giving up your own rights to be served, not using authority for your own advantage

3. *How do these passages help us appreciate God's grace toward us?*

   Jesus is deserving and worthy of worship, yet he gave up his rights so we could be saved from death and have a new relationship with God.

THE ROLE OF THE HUSBAND (10 minutes)

1. *How many times does some form of the word* love *appear in this passage?*

   Seven times

2. *To what is a husband's love compared?*

   To Christ's love for the church

3. *In this most detailed instruction to husbands found in the Bible, why do you think Paul doesn't provide a list of responsibilities, but instead emphasizes the husband's call to love?*

   Whatever the husband's responsibilities are they must be founded on the love of Christ.

4. *In what ways can you begin to sacrifice for your wife so that she is loved and cared for as Christ loves and cares for us?*

   Sometimes when we think of loving sacrificially we envision martyrs being burned at the stake. Maybe a few husbands will have the opportunity to protect their wives from a bullet or shove them out of the way of a speeding car, but if you start looking for them your day is filled with ways to sacrificially love your wife. Maybe it's as simple as loading the dishwasher, tucking the kids into bed, or throwing a load of laundry into the dryer, or as simple as taking a few minutes to pray with her over something she's anxious about.

5. *Name some ways that a husband can go wrong in his exercise of authority.*

   Some examples:

   By hindering his wife's growth. A husband might use his authority in a controlling way and insist on making all the decisions. But doing this will not encourage either partner to grow in wisdom. A desire for control may expose a lack of trust in God. It may be a way to combat fear. Do you fear rejection? Do you micromanage out of a sense of insecurity? Do you fear that if you don't personally hold everything together it will all fall apart? Or is control more about feeding appetites for power or simply having things done for your own convenience? To the extent that you use authority to manage your own fears and feed your own desires, you are subverting Jesus' authority and enthroning yourself.

   By not knowing his wife. A husband can't make wise decisions about how to love his wife if he doesn't know her—her hopes, dreams, fears, desires, strengths, and weaknesses. Patient, careful communication allows a couple to build unity in marriage and reveals unilateral decision making for the failure to love that it really is.

THE ROLE OF THE WIFE (10 minutes)

1. *What are wives instructed to do? What does this look like? (Consider again, Jesus' own example.)*

   Submit to their husbands as to the Lord. Respect their husbands

2. *In submitting to their husbands, to whom are wives ultimately submitting? (vs. 22)*

   God himself. Paul urges wives to accept and respect their husband's authority as a way of entrusting themselves to Christ's care and authority over them, just as the entire church must do. God asks wives to allow their husbands to love and care for them, and to trust that God will care for them even when their husbands do not.

3. *Where does the power to submit come from? (vs. 18)*

   The Holy Spirit

199

4. *List some temptations to sin in the area of submitting to authority.*

   The most common is simply to reject or undermine authority.

   Leader notes: Psalm 13 provides a quick study in honest, open communication. It may be startling to think that David could be that honest with God without being considered disrespectful. But David is being submissive in a godly way. He's being honest in a way that honors who God really is. David is saying, in effect, "God, I know that you're truly good and I'm having trouble understanding why you're not doing things differently. Help!"

   Be careful that your understanding of submission isn't missing important elements of love. For example, some equate correction with disrespect, but as we've seen, the Bible considers correction one of the most basic responsibilities of love. Your obligation to love your husband is certainly not less than your obligation to a "neighbor." So respectfully correcting your husband is part of loving him.

REMEMBER YOUR COMMON CALLING
(10 minutes)

Peter begins his instruction to both wives and husbands (3:1, 7) using the phrase: "in the same way." To what does this phrase refer? In the same way as what?

This phrase refers to Christ's service described in 1 Peter 2. Jesus is the head of his people, and he submits to authority. As Jesus led and submitted, he endured great hardship. But he trusted God to work through even the most difficult moments. Rather than lashing out at the sins of others, Jesus displayed love, mercy, and patience.

Homework for Unit 9

Unit 10: Keep Your Eyes on the Prize

Leader suggestion: Optional: Gather some blank note cards and envelopes for the activity at the end of the lesson.

Lesson 10

OPENING (10 minutes)

PRACTICING HOPE (15 minutes)

1. *In Matthew 6, what is Jesus cautioning us not to put our hope in?*

   Treasures on earth; material possessions

2. *What can happen to our earthly treasures?*

   They can be destroyed or stolen.

3. *What is the danger of placing our hope in earthly things?*

   If your life is devoted to acquiring and enjoying wealth, for example, what will happen when you lose the very thing you've based your life on? What happens when an identity thief ruins your credit, your house is destroyed in a flood, or the stock market collapses? If you have given your heart to those things, they have become your treasure. Your heart will suffer the same fate as your possessions. The flood that wipes out your home will wipe out your heart. The thief that makes off with your wealth also makes off with your heart.

4. *What should we set our hearts on?*

   Treasure in heaven. Pleasing God. When Jesus returns he will bring our reward with him.

5. *What do you think of when you think of heavenly treasure?*

   Ultimately, Jesus is our treasure. It is his redemptive work that in the end will remake everything in heaven and on earth, including our own hearts and relationships. When you think of treasure that way, you realize that you already have received a down payment on it. In the here and now, you have an intimate relationship with Jesus, and his Spirit lives inside of you. You are connected with him at all times and can seek encouragement or share your thoughts, desires, and fears any time you choose to. That's where you should be placing your hope.

7. *In what ways is the kingdom of heaven hidden?*

    Jesus' work is often subtle, working change in and through us over time, and allowing for many ups and downs.

8. *To what lengths did the man in Matthew 13 go to gain the treasure?*

    It cost him all he had.

9. *What was the man's attitude when he realized that the treasure lay within his grasp?*

    He was filled with joy.

YOU'VE GOTTA HAVE FAITH (15 minutes)

1. *What is it we hope for as Christians?*

    Many answers will be acceptable here: salvation, being rewarded, finding it was all worth it, hope for God to be faithful to his promises.

2. *What are things we currently do not see?*

    Many answers are acceptable here: we do not see Jesus; how everything fits together; we do not always see God's purposes or presence.

3. *Was the faith the "ancients were commended for" (vs. 2) an emotion or an action? (If you can, read the entire chapter in your Bible.) Explain.*

    In the examples in Hebrews 11, God's people are engaged in taking action. Noah builds a boat on dry land in a world that has never seen rain. Abraham and his family leave civilization and comfort to take a journey to a new home they've never seen. The list goes on. These are men and women who take action, and the Bible helps us see how their actions make a difference. Note that their actions are not panicked reactions, rash grabs at control, or prideful attempts to be heroic; they are responses to God's promises and a belief in his activity.

4. *Seeing faith as a decision, how might it play an important role in your marriage?*

    Faith is about believing what God says is true even when experiences and emotions and God's promises don't seem to add up. You will feel bad in the difficult moments of marriage. Being called to faith isn't a rebuke for negative emotions or an exhortation to positive thinking, but a call to focus on God's promises, love, and faithfulness even when they aren't visible. True faith is most obvious when it empowers you to action that is opposite to your emotions. Doing what you feel like doing doesn't take faith. Faith, being focused on the unseen person and activity of God, often calls you to move against your fears, doubts, disappointment, and anger. Rather than denying these feelings, you have the freedom to acknowledge them and ask for help. Your actions can be governed by your relationship with God. The power of that relationship, and your faith in that relationship, becomes most obvious to you when it moves you to do what you believe God is calling you to do instead of what you feel like doing.

FAITH AND ACTION (10 minutes)

1. *How did Israel feel physically when God called them to go to battle with Amalek? Did Israel feel up to the task?*

   They were weary, worn out, and afraid. They had been slaves for generations. They weren't likely to have been trained to fight.

2. *Why does Moses stand on the hill with the staff outstretched? (Read Exodus 4:1–5.)*

   God had given Moses his staff earlier as a symbol of his presence and power.

3. *What determines the outcome of the battle?*

   Exodus 17:11 says, "As long as Moses held up his hands, the Israelites were winning, but whenever he lowered his hands, the Amalekites were winning."

4. *What does it mean that God requires Moses to hold his arms up in order for the battle to be won?*

   The most obvious meaning is that God is the one who was ultimately fighting the Amalekites and determining the outcome of the battle. On the one hand, God's people couldn't afford to believe the battle was entirely in their own hands. If they did, they probably wouldn't even have had enough courage to step onto the battlefield. On the other hand, they couldn't afford to sit on the sidelines and just see what God would do. God called them to action with the understanding that he would work through them to determine the outcome.

5. *Describe how Moses, in this story, is a picture of Jesus.*

   The account of Israel's battle with the Amalekites reminds us that *we* have a Savior whose arms don't get tired.

FOCUSING ON THE REAL STORY—GOD'S WORK (10 minutes)

1. *What was God's purpose in bringing hardships on his people?*

   God used hardships to reveal their hearts. In the wilderness there were no Egyptians to blame and no distractions that might allow them to avoid the subject. It was just Israel, God, and the desert.

2. *What is God's purpose for us in our own sufferings?*

   As was the case for Israel, God allows us to suffer to expose what lies hidden in our hearts—who we really are and what we really need.

3. *In verse 3 what does God say he was teaching the Israelites?*

   "That man does not live on bread alone but on every word that comes from the mouth of the Lord."

SOMETHING TO THINK ABOUT

Leader suggestion: In closing, pass out note cards and envelopes. Have participants address the envelopes to themselves and write out on the note cards what they hope will have changed in their marriages two to three months from now. (Encourage participants to focus on their own behaviors.) Have participants place what they wrote in the self-addressed envelope. Collect the envelopes and mail them out in two to three months.

Homework for Unit 10